THE HIDDEN TREASURE

SPIRITUAL PEARLS

Contemporary writers address timeless elements of Christian spirituality:

1. *I Believe in Eternal Life,* Carlo Maria Martini
2. *The Hidden Treasure: The art of searching within,* José Tolentino Mendonça
3. *Why Pray How to Pray,* Enzo Bianchi

The Hidden Treasure

❖

THE ART OF SEARCHING WITHIN

JOSÉ TOLENTINO MENDONÇA

Foreword by Cardinal Gianfranco Ravasi
President, Pontifical Council for Culture

ST PAULS

Originally published in Portugal as *O Tesouro Escondido, Para uma Arte da Procura Interior* © 2011, Instituto Missionário Filhas de São Paulo – Paulinas Editora, Rua Francisco Salgado Zenha, 11 – 2685-332 Prior Velho – Portugal www.paulinas.pt

English translation by Mary John Ronayne, OP, copyright © 2012 by Paulinas Editora.

Library of Congress Cataloging-in-Publication Data

Mendonça, José Tolentino.
   [Tesouro escondido. English]
   The hidden treasure: the art of searching within / José Tolentino Mendonça ; foreword by Cardinal Gianfranco Ravasi, president, Pontifical Council for Culture.
     pages cm.
   Includes bibliographical references and index.
   ISBN 978-0-8189-1365-5
   1. Spiritual life—Catholic Church. 2. Spirituality—Catholic Church. I. Title.
   BX2350.3.M45513 2013
   248.4'82—dc23

                        2013028179

Produced and designed in the United States of America by the Fathers and Brothers of the Society of St. Paul, 2187 Victory Boulevard, Staten Island, New York 10314-6603 as part of their communications apostolate.

ISBN 978-0-8189-1365-5

Printing Information:

Current Printing - first digit	1	2	3	4	5	6	7	8	9	1 0

Year of Current Printing - first year shown

2014	2015	2016	2017	2018	2019	2020	2021	2022	2023

What dwelling shall receive me? in what vale
Shall be my harbor? underneath what grove
Shall I take up my home?

William Wordsworth

Contents

Foreword

Together with the gift of faith, God also gave to José Tolentino Mendonça – priest, theologian and poet – the ability to sing it. An interweaving of faith and poetry, then. These pages offer us a clear example of this. In fact, they are filled with the iridescence of the images, the thrust of important and incisive words, the freshness of the style, the power of the poetry. But they all have their roots in the Bible, the bedrock of faith, and reach out to the Beyond and the divine Other. In fact, the book's title refers us to one of Jesus' 35 parables, that of the treasure hidden in a field (Mt 13:44). However, it is the subtitle that gives us the strongest thread in the whole volume: "The art of searching within."

The key term is *quest, search, enquiry,* a term which, because of its dynamic nature and deep significance for all cultures and spiritualities, prompted Plato to put this surprising remark on the lips of his teacher in the *Apology of Socrates:* "Life without enquiry is not worth living." One of the dominant notes in the Psalter is precisely that of "seeking the face of the Lord." "When shall I come and behold the face of God?" is the anguished cry of the one praying that poetic and spiritual jewel, Psalm 42, the story of a soul forced to live in exile in a foreign land. Note how the dynamic verbs "to come" and "to see" are interwoven, both being synonyms of "to seek," a term which dominates in many of the psalms.

Holding firmly to this thematic thread, let us go through Fr. José Tolentino's text from the beginning, where Moses, at the sight of the burning bush which was to change his whole life, makes his choice: "I will go closer and see" (Ex 3:3). A few pages further on, we have the parable of the treasure in which "to find something is not yet to possess it." In fact, the finder must first "go and sell all that he has and buy that field." As the poet T.S. Eliot suggests, we need to be "explorers, still moving into another intensity, a further union, a deeper communion." The very "wound" of the sterility, of Abraham's wife, Sarah, is transformed into a journey in which she "follows the path of trust in God's promise." The Providence that guides our steps is indeed "a footprint of God in time" given in order to lead us to "a purpose for history itself." The "questions to be put to grown-ups" are those that are asked "midway upon the journey," as happens in the case of the radical question that Jesus puts to his disciples at the half-way point of his public life (and also of the Gospel): "But who do you say that I am?" (Mt 16:15).

Some Gospel scenes throw light on this grammar of seeking and the spiritual quest. José Tolentino Mendonça presents the obvious and extraordinary episode of the disciples of Emmaus, superimposed, so to speak, onto a journey and an arrival, a seeking and a finding. Equally suggestive is the parable of the coin that is lost and found (Lk 15:8-10) which is set into that mini-Gospel of lost ones, the 15th chapter of the Gospel of St. Luke. Four stages of the journey of quest are identified: light the lamp, sweep out the inner house, seek diligently, rejoice when the goal is reached and what was lost is found. Basing himself on the well-known travel writer, Bruce Chatwin, Mendonça constructs his own "anatomy of restlessness," faith being a journey, and gives a list of the great travelers of the faith.

These range from the nomad Abraham to Moses, who led the march to freedom; from the fugitive Elijah who travelled to Horeb-Sinai to the unwilling migrant Jonah, who only learns the truth about God by going abroad; from Jesus himself who has not even a stone on which to lay his head and who is constantly on the move, down to the disciples who are sent out to the whole world and to Paul, the tireless missionary traveler. Indeed, communion with God is achieved by means of a *prosagogé,* a Greek word used by the Apostle Paul to celebrate the "access," etymologically almost being thrust towards the mystery of light which is God (Rm 5:2; Eph 3:12). The *Our Father,* too, like every prayer, is the experience of a nearness but also of a distance to be overcome. Christ came precisely in order to lead us to the Father, overcoming the distance of transcendence by means of an intimacy to be won when we place our own hands in his.

Other luminous threads are wrapped around the central thread so far discussed, which are gradually unwound throughout this book. I will mention only two. On the one hand, there is the thread of prayer. In addition to the *Our Father,* there is a lovely and intense chapter devoted to the *Magnificat,* "a poem which does not only hymn the promised land but proclaims it," in the words of the Portuguese poet Sophia De Mello Breyner Andresen. The white man's self-centeredness — according to a Native American — "makes God poorer." And Mary chooses the opposite, "magnifying" the Lord, that is recognizing Him and glorifying Him as greater through the lowliness of his handmaid, "servant and poor."

On the other hand, there is the slender but glowing thread of beauty, a reality much loved by Fr. José Tolentino, who is a poet and important cultural representative in his native country, Portugal. Significant from this point of view are the many intense and lovely voices that he evokes in these pages, ranging from the philosopher Kierkegaard to the poet T.S. Eliot; from the fascinating and dramatic testimony of Etty Hillesum to the always moving testimony of Simone Weil; from Claudel to Bonhoeffer, from John of the Cross to Gaudi, from the Greek mystical theologian Cabasilas to Hildegard of Bingen, down to the words of Benedict XVI on beauty ("make your lives places of beauty"). But Christ himself "the fairest of the children of men," as suggested in Psalm 45, remains central, even though, on the cross, he was capable of arousing a feeling of revulsion, forcing us to turn our heads away, as was the case for the Servant of Lord celebrated by the prophet Isaiah (ch. 53).

Beauty, in fact, is not mere aestheticism but rather an open wound which impels us to undertake the quest with which we began, invading and disturbing our lethargy. It is a narrow opening giving access to the Absolute, the Eternal, the Mystery, but only by means of a peep-hole which forces us to project our gaze and sharpen our vision. And so we

come to the final appeal: "Without the attractive beauty of
Christ, Christianity [like the inner life itself] is dry, functional, bureaucratic, ritualistic, an outward bath of conventions to
which our hearts remain impervious... Let us allow ourselves
to be touched, enchanted, fall in love with, be wounded by the
Beauty which God reveals in Jesus."

Cardinal Gianfranco Ravasi
President, Pontifical Council for Culture

Biblical Abbreviations

OLD TESTAMENT

Genesis	Gn	Nehemiah	Ne	Baruch	Ba
Exodus	Ex	Tobit	Tb	Ezekiel	Ezk
Leviticus	Lv	Judith	Jdt	Daniel	Dn
Numbers	Nb	Esther	Est	Hosea	Ho
Deuteronomy	Dt	1 Maccabees	1 M	Joel	Jl
Joshua	Jos	2 Maccabees	2 M	Amos	Am
Judges	Jg	Job	Jb	Obadiah	Ob
Ruth	Rt	Psalms	Ps	Jonah	Jon
1 Samuel	1 S	Proverbs	Pr	Micah	Mi
2 Samuel	2 S	Ecclesiastes	Ec	Nahum	Na
1 Kings	1 K	Song of Songs	Sg	Habakkuk	Hab
2 Kings	2 K	Wisdom	Ws	Zephaniah	Zp
1 Chronicles	1 Ch	Sirach	Si	Haggai	Hg
2 Chronicles	2 Ch	Isaiah	Is	Malachi	Ml
Ezra	Ezr	Jeremiah	Jr	Zechariah	Zc
		Lamentations	Lm		

NEW TESTAMENT

Matthew	Mt	Ephesians	Eph	Hebrews	Heb
Mark	Mk	Philippians	Ph	James	Jm
Luke	Lk	Colossians	Col	1 Peter	1 P
John	Jn	1 Thessalonians	1 Th	2 Peter	2 P
Acts	Ac	2 Thessalonians	2 Th	1 John	1 Jn
Romans	Rm	1 Timothy	1 Tm	2 John	2 Jn
1 Corinthians	1 Cor	2 Timothy	2 Tm	3 John	3 Jn
2 Corinthians	2 Cor	Titus	Tt	Jude	Jude
Galatians	Gal	Philemon	Phm	Revelation	Rv

THE HIDDEN TREASURE

1

❖

God's lamp has not gone out

Let us begin, a little clumsily perhaps, by asking whether our inner world is an onion or a potato. The question makes us smile, it is rather comical but if we let it, in the end it will bring us face to face quite profoundly with our reality. The question can be asked in a kitchen by a child who is discovering the world; it can be asked by a philosopher in his reflections or by a spiritual master. Is our inner world an onion or a potato? Nietzsche, for example, used to say that "everything is interpretation," in other words, there is no nucleus of Being supporting our experience of life, everything is onion skins, points of view, perspectives, interpretations. Beyond that there is nothing else. The Christian vision of the world is certainly on the side of the potato, because it maintains that, *even if it is hidden by a scab or a veil, it is a reality which is solid and vital.*

The truth is that even though we accept that life is a potato, we very often live as if it were an onion. We live on opinions, on partial and provisional truths, on emotions; we live appearances and fashions as if life consisted in these. We wear ourselves out displaying outer coverings and layers without a center which would, in fact, allow us to grasp the full meaning. A contemporary writer, Susan Sontag, says that our existence is as it were entangled in this endless stream of interpretations which distract us from the real journey. We do not live within ourselves, but are carried away by ideas, points of view, the absolutizing of circumstances, more and more outer coverings. In her view, the most urgent task would be to *purify and deepen* our meanings, learning to see more clearly, to feel more deeply, to listen more attentively. It is this that is most important in the spiritual life also. Simone Weil wrote: "The key is the realization that prayer consists of attention. It is the orientation of all the attention of which the soul is capable towards God. The quality of the attention counts for much in the quality of the prayer."

At a time of reflection on the interior life, we feel the challenge of paying attention, of watchfulness which is nothing other than trustingly to *see more clearly, feel more deeply and listen more attentively to what God reveals in us.* Let us get away from our onion-like confusion. The Bible which, for believers, is an authentic handbook introducing us to the spiritual adventure, offers us many examples of how necessary it is to recover this inner attention in order to be able to hear God who is speaking to us. Let us take two texts for our reflection.

To begin with, the episode marking the beginning of the call of Moses in the desert:

> Moses was keeping the flock of his father-in-law,
> Jethro, the priest of Midian, and he led his flock to

2

the west side of the wilderness, and came to Horeb, the mountain of God. And the angel of the Lord appeared to him in a flame of fire out of the midst of a bush; and he looked and lo, the bush was burning, yet it was not consumed. And Moses said: "I will go closer and see this great sight, why the bush is not burnt." When the Lord saw that he went closer to see, God called to him out of the bush, "Moses, Moses!" And he said: "Here I am!" (Ex 3:1-4)

Let us look at the verb Moses uses: *"I will go closer."* In other words, I will go as close as possible, I want to get right inside; I want, as it were, to plunge into what I see before me. When he ceased to be satisfied with partial appearances, things seen at a distance and hidden in the mist, when he wished with all the power of his being to have clear answers to the questions in his heart, the Book of Exodus tells us that "the Lord saw him... and called him." The Lord is waiting to call us. Let us go right up to him. Let us leave aside a vague spirituality where we are scattered spectators. Let us seek the One who confirms, the One who imparts solidity to our desire.

Let us learn also from the account of the call of the prophet Samuel:

Now the boy Samuel was ministering to the Lord under Eli. And the word of the Lord was rare in those days: there were no frequent visions. At that time Eli, whose sight had begun to grow dim so that

he could not see, was lying down in his own place;
the lamp of God had not yet gone out, and Samuel was lying down within the temple of the Lord,
where the ark of God was. Then the Lord called,
"Samuel! Samuel!" and he said "Here I am" and ran
to Eli, and said, "Here I am, for you called me." But
he said, "I did not call; lie down again." So he went
and lay down. And the Lord called again, "Samuel!"
And Samuel arose and went to Eli, and said, "Here
I am, for you called me." But he said, "I did not call,
my son; lie down again." Now Samuel did not yet
know the Lord, and the word of the Lord had not
yet been revealed to him. And the Lord called Samuel again the third time. And he arose and went to
Eli and said, "Here I am, for you called me." Then
Eli perceived that the Lord was calling the boy.
Therefore Eli said to Samuel, "Go, lie down; and
if he calls you, you shall say, 'Speak, Lord, for your
servant is listening.'" So Samuel went and lay down
in his place. And the Lord came and stood forth,
calling as at other times, "Samuel! Samuel!" And
Samuel said "Speak, for your servant is listening."
(1 S 3:1-10)

"And the word of the Lord was rare in those days: there
were no frequent visions." These words strike us as a realistic
assessment of our own experience. Our daily lives, too, have
become rarefied, fragmentary and remote in relation to God's
presence. However, let us emphasize the extraordinary com-

ment made by the sacred author: "The lamp of God had not yet gone out." God is faithful to human beings and to history. Even in situations and in periods tossed about by winds and turbulence, our trust is placed in that: "The lamp of God had not gone out."

The text tells us that Samuel did not yet know the Lord. What about ourselves? Do we know Him? Samuel hears someone calling him, but reacts badly because he thinks that it is Eli who was summoning him. And this continues until he is helped to *go back to the Lord* and to pray: *"Speak, Lord, for your servant is listening."* The Lord does not cease to speak to us, but we need a spiritual pedagogy which will help us to direct towards God our inner feelings and thoughts. "To turn towards the Lord" is the literal meaning of the word "conversion." The way for the believer is this pedagogical exercise and practice of conversion, this real opportunity to turn aside offered to us by God. In the darkness or the sunshine of our lives, in the days that we are actually living, let us pray with all our hearts the prayer of Samuel: *"Speak, Lord, for your servant is listening."*

One last thought: let us beg for the gift of silence to accompany us on our journey. As the poem of Sophia de Mello Breyner Andresen puts it:

Deixai-me limpo	Leave clean for me
O ar dos quartos	the air in the rooms
E liso	and smooth
O branco das paredes	the whiteness of the walls
Deixai-me com as coisasa	Leave me with everything
Fundadas no silêncio.	bathed in silence.

Our spiritual senses open up and ripen better in silence. Let us plunge into it the mark of our footsteps. This is the unanimous advice given to us by Christian spiritual masters to enable us to make the transition from the onion to the humble but solid and life-giving potato. Arsenius' advice was this: "Flee. Be silent. Keep recollected." Poemen guaranteed: "If you are silent, you will have peace wherever you live." In the first half of the 7th century, John Climacus wrote: "The friend of silence draws near to God and, by secretly conversing with Him, is enlightened by God." Isaac of Nineveh's prescription for those who sought him out was: "More than all things love silence: it brings you a fruit that the tongue cannot describe.... Within our very silence is born something that draws us into deeper silence. May God give you an experience of this 'something' that is born of silence."

We must not fear the silence which is the breath of the interior life, for we are called to embrace it. I love that remark of the Italian designer Bruno Munari: "A tree is a seed which grows slowly and in silence."

2

❖

Light your lamp

Or what woman, having ten silver coins, if she los-
es one coin, does not light a lamp and sweep the
house and seek diligently until she finds it? And
when she has found it, she calls together her friends
and neighbors, saying: "Rejoice with me, for I have
found the coin which I had lost." Just so, I tell you,
there is joy before the angels of God over one sinner
who repents. (Lk 15:8-10)

This parable occurs in chapter 15 of the Gospel according to
St. Luke and is like two others which are better known and
used more frequently in the Liturgy, namely the parables of
the Lost Sheep and of the Prodigal Son. For this reason, this
important chapter of St. Luke's Gospel has been described as
"the gospel of loss." The experience of loss marks our existence
in various ways. We get lost from the Father and from the Father's house. We get lost from our brothers and sisters. We lose
ourselves in time and in the sheepfold. We lose ourselves....
There is a Negro spiritual which goes like this: "Sometimes I

feel like a motherless child/Sometimes I feel like a motherless child, a long way from home."

When we draw up the balance-sheet of the particular period in our lives that we are currently living, it is naturally our losses that come to the surface of our hearts. Jesus helps us to find ourselves without masking or diminishing the dramatic nature of the things that have gone wrong but showing us that they can be turned into opportunities for "going closer" in the knowledge of God and of ourselves. "I will go closer and see this great sight, why the bush is not burnt" (Ex 3:3). The paradox of God's love is this: through the things that we lose we learn, for instance, the extent to which the shepherd is prepared to go in search of the sheep that is lost. He searches everywhere "until he finds it" (Lk 15:5). We are left with this unforgettable picture of the Father who almost literally "covers with kisses" (Lk 15:20) the wounds of a failure to love in both his sons.

In this context, the little parable in Luke 15:8-10 is especially significant. Unlike the others, it describes the loss of something within, almost personal; part of the treasure is lost within the person's own house. I think we all know about this, without elaborate explanations. Notice that we do not lose everything, or even the greater part of something. Of the ten silver coins that she possessed, the woman had lost only one. It almost does not count. But the person who experiences this loss realizes what it means: a cooling-off, a diminution, a break in the wholeness of life, in the overall unity of the "yes" of love of which we are made. It is akin to what the Spirit criticized in the Church at Ephesus, in the Book of Revelation: "I

8

know your works, your toil and your patient endurance…. You are enduring patiently and bearing up for my name's sake, and you have not grown weary. But I have this against you that you have abandoned the love you had at first" (Rv 2:2-4). Having lost one coin, life goes on, but it is not the same as before.

Most of the time, when we sin it is not only that we allow ourselves to be imprisoned by concrete evils, but rather that we let slip a demanding and vigilant high point, the prophetic and integral measure of the Kingdom in ourselves, and then we settle for that, as if we had not really lost anything. This is a typical spiritual problem of our adult lives, of a committed Christianity, in which we are beset by temptations to cynicism and to letting go of "the love we had at first." We are quicker at beginning to look for keys or money that we don't know where they have got to…. In this way we grow accustomed to a diminished, softened, spiritual life, made up of half shades and half-truths, and we lack the courage needed for full truths. For the moment, we have stopped living for God and for God alone. But is this what we want?

The poet Sophia de Mello Breyner Andresen has written: "A half-truth is like living in half a room/Earning half pay/It is like being entitled/to half a life." What nourishes us and how do we live? Do we live to the full or have we settled for a half-life?

Relearn the art of searching

The woman had ten silver coins and, having lost one of them, she did not simply decide that at any rate she still had nine. Instead, she decided to look for the part of her treasure that she had lost. "It is you, O Lord, who are my hope, my trust, O Lord, since my youth" in the words of Psalm 70(1). We are dealing here with a youthfulness of soul. The woman did not blame anyone for her loss, she did not look for scapegoats, she did not sulk or get depressed... but at the same time she did not just settle down with her arms folded. What about us? Maybe we still have nine or seven or five or three coins left.... And we can try to console ourselves and deceive ourselves with what is left, telling ourselves that we do not really need another life, a different kind of freshness, a complete heart. The first moment of reconciliation is the interior decision that prompts us precisely to practice once again the art of seeking, the art of wholeness. "If you want to be great, be of one piece," said Fernando Pessoa. And it is clear that the great challenge of the spiritual life is not to be great but to be all of a piece. To be ourselves.

The little parable of Luke 15:8-10 offers us a kind of pedagogy of wholeness, presenting us with a journey in four stages:

Light the lamp

In the darkness I see nothing; all I do is to remain in the dark which tends to get darker, and to confuse us. For this reason, I need God's light to enable me to see. "God's lamp had not gone out" (1 S 3:3). In the spiritual assessments that we make of our lives, the important thing is not so much the mere examination with our human eyes. As St. Paul explains so well: "Now we see in a mirror dimly" (1 Cor 13:12). As we read in the Prologue to St. John's Gospel, the Word is "the true light that enlightens everyone on coming into the world" (Jn 1:9). Let us light the Word of God in our hearts, taking Jesus as our model in everything: "For in you is the source of life, and in your light we see light" (Ps 35(6):9). "What a lot of time we have lost, what a lot of work put off on account of our lack of attention to this point! Everything is to be defined starting with Christ," as Pope Benedict XVI firmly reminded his audience during his most recent visit to Portugal.

May Isaiah's promise that is echoed in the Gospels be fulfilled: "The people who sat in darkness have seen a great light, and for those who sat in the region and shadow of death light has dawned" (Mt 4:16). Let us make Peter's prayer our own: "Lord, to whom should we go? You have the words of eternal life" (Jn 6:68).

To sweep

To sweep is an active verb. I do not simply stop at bewailing what has happened. I start "to sweep," to clean, to transform, to let some light in. The dust and disorder of all sorts of things have piled up. I often think about the tiny planet that the Little Prince, the character created by Saint-Exupéry, had come from.

> On the planet where the little prince lived – as on
> all planets – there are good plants and bad plants.
> In consequence, there were good seeds from good

plants and bad seeds from bad plants. But seeds are invisible. They sleep deep in the heart of the earth's darkness, until someone among them is seized with the desire to awaken. Then this little seed will stretch itself and begin – timidly at first – to push a charming little sprig inoffensively upward towards the sun. If it is only a sprout of radish or the sprig of a rose-bush, one would let it grow wherever it might wish. But when it is a bad plant, one must destroy it as soon as possible, the very first instant that one recognizes it. Now there were some terrible seeds on the planet that was the home of the little prince; and these were the seeds of the baobab. The soil of that planet was infested with them. A baobab is something you will never, never be able to get rid of if you attend to it too late. It spreads over the entire planet. It bores clear through it with its roots. And if the planet is too small, and the baobabs are too many, they split it in pieces.... "It is a question of discipline," the little prince said to me later on. "When you've finished your own toilet in the morning, then it is time to attend to the toilet of your planet, just so, with the greatest care. Sometimes there is no harm in putting off a piece of work until another day. But when it is a matter of baobabs, that always means a catastrophe. Once there was a planet that was inhabited by a lazy man. He neglected three little bushes...."

Even though our lives seem to be a tiny planet,

there is a lot of work to be done every day. Basically, it is a question of accepting that life demands of me, here and now, an energetic "yes." I have to struggle to be myself. If I do not sweep my house, it will cease to be habitable; it will cease to be mine....

There is a curious remark in Paul Claudel's diary: "The spiritual life is not a question of doors but of windows." In fact, it is not a question of ceasing to be the person I am, or of looking for a solution outside of myself, but rather of opening the windows and letting God's air in, letting the wind of the Spirit blow through it.

To search diligently

Our search for conversion is not outside of ourselves. There is no question of our creating a table or compiling a list of our faults and failings as if there were no connection between them... and as if the vital connecting link were not what I am in myself. There are underlying reasons and interior obstacles in us that need to be identified. "Seek diligently," advises the woman in the parable. We too need to go to the bottom of things and find the root of whatever it is that is devitalizing us spiritually. It may well be an enormous, a frightening fear.... Perhaps it is a fundamental failure to trust in the love of God. Maybe I lack confidence and for this reason have very little courage. Perhaps it all stems from an inability to forgive, that is, to cover the wounds and humiliations I have suffered with the conviction that love is the only thing that is good. I seek diligently. God grant that we may say with Edith Stein (St. Teresa Benedicta of the Cross): "My search for the truth was indeed a prayer."

Rejoice with me

Our reconciliation would be incomplete if it did not result in a return of joy. Very often, our joy is circumstantial: we tell or we hear a lovely story, something amusing happens, etc. But the woman is speaking of something different when she says: "Rejoice with me." There is a real overflowing joy for the things that God brings about in us, a surprising and paschal revitalization of our lives. Joy, then, is not an outer garment, but we ourselves become a cause of joy for one another, a joy that is experienced not only on earth but reaches to heaven itself.

3

❖

A hidden treasure

The kingdom of heaven is like a treasure hidden in a field, which a man found and covered up; then in his joy he goes and sells all that he has and buys that field. Again, the kingdom of heaven is like a merchant in search of fine pearls who, on finding one pearl of great price, went and sold all that he had and bought it. (Mt 13:44-46)

Like the man in Jesus' parable, we find a treasure: God's love. We know where it is, but we do not yet allow ourselves to be fully possessed by it, we continue to live in a state of tension in our endeavor to allow it to become really present in us. This is the path travelled by faith throughout history, a path trodden in hope which never comes to an end. Pope Benedict XVI has written incisively about this hope in the Introduction to his encyclical, *Spe Salvi*:

According to our Christian faith, redemption is not simply a given. Redemption is offered to us in the sense that we have been given hope, trustworthy hope, by virtue of which we can face our present. The present, even if it is arduous, can be lived and accepted if it leads towards a goal, if we can be sure of this goal, and if this goal is great enough to justify the effort of the journey.

The parable is very true to life: to find something is only the beginning, undoubtedly great in itself and galvanizing us into action, but to find something is not yet to possess it. What is it that we lack in order to become the owners of our treasure? According to the story as Jesus told it, we have to hide the treasure again in the place where we found it, then go and sell everything we possess before returning to purchase the field or the pearl. We might well think that a merchant "who is seeking good pearls" would already have whatever he needed in order to purchase them at once as soon as he found them. But the parable warns us, precisely, against this "spur of the moment" mentality, consisting of very impulsive emotions. Faith is a history of fidelity which is slowly built up, not the mere enthusiasm of a moment.

We must be pleased to have found our treasure. However, it would be naive on our part, or even a foolish mistake, to think that we already possess it. Finding it puts us once again back on the road in search of it. So often the spiritual life turns out to be precisely this: the painstaking, prolonged, patient and earnest search for that which or the One whom we have already found. We would not be looking for God unless we had already found him, but the longing for an unconditional love makes us realize that the first encounter is only the beginning. Nothing has been settled because everything broadens out. This was the lesson that Peter learnt from Jesus when, thinking that he was reaching the utmost heights, he asked whether we were required to forgive others up to seven times. "I do not say to you seven times, but seventy times seven" (Mt 18:22), was the reply he was given. There is always a new horizon that God opens before our humanity. In the words of Cardinal Newman, faith is always *developing* and, for this reason, a maturing of the soul for Truth. "Here, on earth, to live is to change, and to be perfect is to have changed often" (Cardinal Newman).

What does the merchant in the parable do? He goes back to hide the treasure. What a strange thing to do, we might think, yet it is something filled with spiritual wisdom. If we begin showing off the treasure before we fully possess it, we are putting it in danger and may lose what we thought was ours too soon. The seed which sprang up immediately is the one that fell on rocky ground where it had no depth of soil; so that when the sun rose it was scorched and, since it had no root, it withered away (Mk 4:5-6). This happens with love, too. We can display one or other subject that interests us, but a true love needs to mature in the silence of intimacy. St. John of the Cross's spiritual experience led him describe love as follows:

> How tame and loving
> Your memory rises in my breast,
> Where secretly only you live.

For this Saint, "what we most need in order to make progress is to silence the appetite and the tongue before this great God, for the language that He hears best is that of silent love." If we rush to expose our love to the light too soon, it weakens, gets mixed up with vanity, becomes yet another of our trophies and runs the risk of becoming trivialized. Kierkegaard's advice is relevant here: "Allowing a secret to mature is a delightful occupation."

Love's wish is for hiddenness. The beloved in the Song of Songs confesses about her loved one: "With great delight I sat in his shadow" (Sg 2:3). And her prayer is an appeal for love: "Draw me after you. Let us make haste! The king has brought me into his chambers" (Sg 1:4). In a way, the author of the Letter to the Colossians extends this situation to all Christians when he writes: "For you have died and your life is hidden with Christ in God" (Col 3:3). The treasure needs to be hidden if we really wish to possess it. It is interesting to remember that the Fathers of the Desert used to say that a Christian's one and only wish was to live "as a person who does not exist, who is invisible." We live in the world and in it we have our commitments, our mission, but we do not belong to it (Jn 15:19). This kind of affective withdrawal, this hidden life, is essential. "Where your treasure is, there will your heart be also" (Lk 12:34). But where is this treasure of ours?

It is impossible to live the spiritual life without solitude. Solitude is to keep a time and a place for God and for God alone. Jesus used to withdraw and hide himself from everybody in order to pray (Mk 1:35). In this place of withdrawal, Jesus became free to know the Father and to take possession of the treasure which this knowledge entails. For this reason, the deeds that he accomplished were not his, the will he sought to carry out was not his alone, nor the words that he communicated: "My food (we can read 'my treasure') is to do the will of him who sent me" (Jn 4:34).

Jesus' advice to his disciples was that they should seek the Father who sees in secret:

> When you pray, you must not be like the hypocrites; for they love to stand in the synagogues and at the street corners, that they may be seen. Truly, I say to you, they have their reward. But when you pray, go into your room and shut the door and pray to your Father who is in secret, and your Father who sees in secret will repay you. (Mt 6:5-6)

When we live in order to be seen, we falsify the profound truth towards which our life should be tending. When we live on activity alone and its results, we become possessive and are less able to be welcoming and to share. In solitude, however, when we enter "into our innermost room and we close the door," we can slowly strip off the illusion of possession and dominion and discover deep down in ourselves that the spiritual life does not consist in a victory to be won, but in a gift to be shared. It is precisely when we are most alone, when we are most ourselves, without subterfuges or evasions, that God reveals himself as being closer to us. In this we have an experience of God as loving Father who knows us better than we know ourselves. Let us recall the intense and illuminating words in St. Augustine's *Confessions*:

> Late have I loved you, O Beauty, so ancient and so new, late have I loved you! And behold, you were within me and I was outside, and there I sought for you, and in my deformity I rushed headlong into the well-formed things that you have made. You were with me, and I was not with you. Those outer beauties held me far from you, yet if they had not been in you, they would not have existed at all. You called, and cried out to me, and broke open my deafness: you shone forth upon me and you scattered my blindness. You breathed fragrance, and I drew in my breath and I now pant for you. I tasted, and I hunger and thirst; you touched me, and I burned for your peace. (*Confessions*, X, XXVII)

In our place of withdrawal, we discover the Spirit that has been given to us. The sufferings and battles that we encounter in our solitude will gradually turn into a road leading to hope, as it leads us to the spring of hope which is the presence of God in our lives. In solitude, we are led to the truth, and we understand that we are what God makes us to be. There is an acceptance which overcomes fear: "There is no fear in love, but perfect love casts out fear" (Jn 4:18). Solitude then becomes a place of conversion. The truth is that it is in the light of the presence of God that we see what we are.

What is it that we really wish for? When we stop in order to listen as attentively as possible to our soul, the word that we hear most often is the word "communion." Communion means "union with." God gave us a heart which yearns for communion and, without it, our heart grows restless and weak. The great temptation that assails us is to doubt our wish for communion. The person in the parable is a great example for us: "In his joy he goes and sells all that he has and buys that field." We have in him an image of perfect communion, the communion which mortgages to the full the whole of our being. This is love: being stripped, choosing and allowing oneself to be handed over. In the Eucharistic words of Jesus: "This is my body which is given for you" (Lk 22:19), we have a proof and an account of love which we are now called upon to live.

4

❖

Old men ought to be explorers

There is a poem by T.S. Eliot which says:

> Old men ought to be explorers....
> We must be still and still moving
> Into another intensity
> A further union, a deeper communion
> ...
> In my end is my beginning. [*East Coker, V*]

"Old men ought to be explorers." Since the beginning, the entire history of salvation is an antidote to the tendency to give up trying. Taken as a whole, the Bible describes more springs than autumns, and some of those springs were very late and almost unlooked-for. "I will pour out my spirit on all human beings. Your sons and your daughters shall prophesy, and your old people shall dream dreams" (Jl 3:1). Is it possible for old people to dream dreams? Normally, it is thought that dreams belong to the beginning stages of life. As we get older we are condemned to make a tally of alarms, precautions and fears.

"Old men ought to be explorers" – the Bible knows this. Let us have a fresh look at the story of Abraham. In Genesis 12, we read:

> Now the Lord said to Abraham, "Go from your country and your kindred and your father's house to the land that I will show you. And I will make of you a great nation, and I will bless you, and make your name great, so that you will be a blessing. I will bless those who bless you, and him who curses you I will curse. And by you all the families of the earth shall bless themselves." So Abraham went, as the Lord had told him... Abraham was seventy-five years old when he departed from Haran. (Gn 12:1-4)

Called by God to begin a new history when he thought his own was already at an end, Abraham was to experience this word as an unlooked-for challenge to go out of himself, to overcome his own personal as well as his sociological context. When God takes the initiative, those concerned break not only with the geographical and familial context which previously constituted their entire security, but also with what this meant: the protection of a citizenship, of a stable family framework, of a sense of belonging. One's life appeared to be settled. Now, faith begins to be, precisely, a challenge to go beyond the individual's own personal way of living his or her life, or at any rate the supposedly definitive forms which we have created for living it, and to open ourselves, right to the end, to the impact of the surprise of God. Faith cuts us free from our installations so that we can live in dependence on God. There are no spiritual car parks. What there is, however, is an unceasing call to experience the following out of a Promise that is greater than ourselves.

Let us compare this text of Genesis 12:1-4 with that other biblical passage which so clearly describes our tendency to conformism that we find in the Song of Songs:

> I slept, but my heart was awake. Hark! My beloved is knocking. "Open to me, my sister, my love, my dove, my perfect one; for my head is wet with dew, my locks with the drops of the night." I had put off my garment, how could I put it on? I had bathed my feet, how could I soil them? (Sg 5:2-3)

That is what we are all like, reluctant to respond to God's calls, more concerned with our own immediate well-being than with the unceasing and demanding toil for the Kingdom. It is no accident that the model of faith is an old man who becomes a traveler, a man who has already retired who takes to the road, a man who in principle ought to be living on the yield from his property and whom God sends to look at the vast sky, as if he were a young man in love, with the future before him, his hands empty and his eyes full. But this is how faith wants us to be, the believer is like this: a pilgrim with poor empty hands and eyes full.

> The Lord said to Abraham in a vision: "Fear not, Abraham, I am your shield; your reward shall be very great." But Abraham said, "O Lord God, what will

you give me, for I continue childless, and the heir of
my house is Eliezer of Damascus?" And he brought
him outside and said, "Look toward heaven, and
number the stars, if you are able to number them."
Then he said to him, "So shall your descendants be."
And Abraham believed the Lord. (Gn 15:1-6)

"And he brought him outside and said, 'Look toward
heaven, and number the stars.'" The Lord leads us out of the
closed circles of our questionings and demonstrations. The
faith is something outside us, a departure from our partial
views of things, a break with our customary perspective.
"Look toward heaven." We need to open the windows, from
which we can see the vast extent of the heavens, look beyond
what our eyes can count, contemplate the immensity which is
a sign of God.

Paul Claudel wrote in his spiritual diary: "The secret of
holiness is to let it be God who is at work and not to place
any obstacle in the way of his will." Then he adds: "It is a *naïve*
trust." The truth is that we place so many barriers in the way
of the call, of the original summons which God places in our
heart. We become calculating to the extreme, with a prudence
that very often is nothing more than an excuse for not accepting and spreading the love of God. "A naive trust." However
old we are, and above all as we advance in years, we need to
recover spiritually the heart of a child.

The disciples came to Jesus saying, "Who is the
greatest in the kingdom of heaven?" Calling to him

a child, he put him in the midst of them and said, "Truly I say to you, unless you turn and become like children, you will never enter the kingdom of heaven. Whoever humbles himself like this child, he is the greatest in the kingdom of heaven." (Mt 18:1-4)

To become little once more, in the astonishment and the confidence with which we live the ways of God.

"Look toward heaven, and number the stars, if you are able to number them." To the very end, let us contemplate the immensity of God; let us fill our eyes with his greatness, with the boundless ocean of his Love. To raise dazzled and trusting eyes to heaven is the attitude of a believer. Let not our eyes, which were made to look at the stars, die through looking down at our boots.

Today, as we read in the Letter to the Hebrews (12:1), we continue to be surrounded by a great cloud of witnesses assuring us of the time and the manner of the adventure of believing. I frequently think of Etty Hillesum, that young woman from Amsterdam who, in the darkest hours of the 20th century, discovered faith in God, and who learned, with such intensity and truth, to pray and to offer herself to work voluntarily in a concentration camp, where in the end she died. Her *Diary* breathes a reviving breath of the Spirit.

Oh God, I thank You for having created me as I am. I thank You for the sense of fulfillment I sometimes have; that fulfillment is after all nothing but being filled with You.

I don't sit here in my peaceful flower-filled room, praising You through Your poets and thinkers. That would be too simple, and in any case I am not as unworldly as my friends so kindly think. Every human being has his own reality, I know that, but I am no fanciful visionary, God, no schoolgirl with a "beautiful soul." I try to face up to Your world, God, not to escape from reality into beautiful dreams – though I believe that beautiful dreams can exist beside the most horrible reality – and I continue to praise Your creation, God, despite everything.

We may of course be sad and depressed by what has been done to us; that is only human and understandable. However: our greatest injury is one we inflict upon ourselves. I find life beautiful, and I feel free. The sky within me is as wide as the one stretching above my head. I believe in God.

And God is not accountable to us for the senseless harm we cause one another. We are accountable to Him! I have already died a thousand deaths in a thousand concentration camps.

I know about everything and am no longer appalled by the latest reports. In one way or another I know it all. And yet I find life beautiful and meaningful. From minute to minute.[1]

---

[1] Etty Hillesum, *An Interrupted Life and Letters from Westerbork* (New York: Henry Holt and Company), 1996.

Old men ought to be explorers

Abraham became a model for all believers. I would like to emphasize two fundamental elements in his faith journey. Abraham lived his faith as a form of hospitality. A clear example of this is the meeting at Mamre:

> The Lord appeared to Abraham by the oaks of Mamre, as he sat at the door of his tent in the heat of the day. He lifted up his eyes and looked, and behold, three men stood in front of him. When he saw them, he ran from the tent door to meet them, and bowed himself to the earth, and said, "My lord, if I have found favor in your sight, do not pass by your servant. Let a little water be brought, and wash your feet, and rest yourselves under the tree, while I fetch a morsel of bread, that you may refresh yourselves, and after that you may pass on – since there must surely be a purpose in your having come to your servant." So they said: "Do as you have said." (Gn 18:1-5)

It was the hottest part of the day, in the desert. Anyone who has ever been there knows that the wisest thing to do at such a time is to seek some kind of shelter and avoid all movement. Now, "Abraham ran from the tent door" to meet the visitors. St. Luke tells us that Mary, too, went with haste into the hill country, to a city of Judah (Lk 1:39). Nobody asked for anything. It was Abraham who took the initiative of welcoming the travelers. We ourselves are often ready to welcome someone, but we wait for a request, a suggestion. Abraham goes forward and this is what constitutes real hospitality. And he does it entirely gratuitously, leaving the other completely free: "When you have refreshed yourselves, you may pass on." His one concern is for us a challenge and a responsibility. "It cannot have been by pure chance that you passed by your servant." There are so many people who pass through our lives.... When it is a question of hospitality, of the service of others, or giving to others, it is important that they should feel that their encounter with us had a purpose.

Abraham's faith is also put to the test. In 1 M 2:52 we read: "Was not Abraham found faithful when tested?" Trial is the place which hones that confidence which is called to be radical, which does not rely on guarantees or signs, but which rests on God alone. God had given to Abraham the son he had been promised, Isaac. Faith, however, is not tied to what our eyes see: God is always God and we must keep our hearts centered on him. Is faith not that mysterious interior exchange in which the I gives place to the Thou, to "through Thee," and "for Thee"? Let us look at another Genesis text:

> After these things, God tested Abraham, and said to him, "Abraham!" And he said, "Here I am." He said, "Take your son, your only son Isaac, whom you love, and go to the land of Moriah, and offer him there as a burnt offering upon one of the mountains of which I shall tell you." So Abraham rose early the next morning, saddled his ass, and took two of his young men with him, and his son Isaac; and he cut the wood for the burnt offering, and arose and went

to the place of which God had told him. On the third day Abraham lifted up his eyes and saw the place afar off. "Stay here with the ass; I and the lad will go yonder and worship, and come again to you." And Abraham took the wood of the burnt offering, and laid it on Isaac his son; and he took in his hand the fire and the knife. So they went both of them together. And Isaac said to his father Abraham, "My father!" And he said, "Here I am, my son." He said, "Behold, the fire and the wood; but where is the lamb for a burnt offering?" Abraham said, "God will provide himself the lamb for a burnt offering, my son." So they went both of them together. When they came to the place of which God had told him, Abraham built an altar there, and laid the wood in order, and bound Isaac his son, and laid him on the altar, upon the wood. Then Abraham put forth his hand, and took the knife to slay his son. But the angel of the Lord called to him from heaven, and said, "Abraham, Abraham!" And he said, "Here I am!" He said, "Do not lay your hand on the lad or do anything to him; for now I know that you fear God seeing you have not withheld your son, your only son, from me." And Abraham lifted up his eyes and looked, and behold, behind him was a ram, caught in a thicket by his horns; and Abraham went and took the ram, and offered it up as a burnt offering instead of his son. So Abraham called the name of the place "The Lord will provide"; as it is said to

this day, "On the mount of the Lord it shall be pro-
vided." (Gn 22:1-14)

The philosopher Sören Kierkegaard interpreted this biblical text as the proclamation of the utter reality of God. In his
Fear and Trembling he wrote, "Truth is not something that is
objectively outside of us that we discover through cold impersonal propositions, but rather it is something we experience
subjectively, inwardly, in a personal way." Faith in God super-
imposes itself on all cultural conventions and all purely human
logics. Faith is that personal trust placed in God which exceeds everything else. Abraham teaches us that faith is a way
of being. Confronted by the incomprehensible plan of God,
he leaves everything else suspended except his relationship
with God. In the depth of our poverty, we too are called to
say: "God will provide."

5

❖

God makes me smile

Trust is a pathway. In most cases, it is a pathway that is not free of questionings, uncertainties and anguished concern. We can truly say that the words of Psalm 22[3] spring from our hearts quite naturally: "No evil would I fear. You are there with your crook and your staff; with these you give me comfort" (v. 4). But making our way through certain stages in our life involves appealing explicitly to the mystery of the Lord's Cross. And this for many reasons: mourning a loved one, an illness, a misunderstanding, an unresolved conflict. With the help of a person in the Bible, let us now reflect on one particular wound, accepting an intimate, symbolic and wide-ranging reading for it. Let us think about sterility.

In biblical times, sterility was regarded as socially shameful, since it was from a fruitful maternity that the Messiah was to be born. But it was also regarded as something that diminished the woman herself or her family. Without posterity, the future was felt to be dark and threatening. This was the dramatic situation in which Abraham found himself, and above all Sarah, his wife. In view of his advanced age, all Abraham could foresee was that a distant relative, Eliezer of Damascus, would be his heir.

We can imagine the cost to Sarah of all this. Anguish causes great suffering and is different from fear. Fear always has an object (whether real or imaginary), and when it is overcome the fear disappears. Anguish, however, is a more intimate feeling. I do not quite know who I am, I am not sure what my role is, I do not feel loved, I am worthless.... In view of all this, I feel in my heart and in my spirit a constant unrest.... To feel lost in this way can result in all kinds of existential uneasiness and depression.

The biblical text is very restrained in relation to the psychological aspect of things, but we can well imagine that Sarah felt let down by her own history. Each one of us is a mixture of strength and fragility, and we ought to rely more on our littleness, our fragility and vulnerability. But we look around us and that is not how things are. Society expects us to be strong, to succeed, to exercise power. And we find ourselves at loggerheads with the wounded image of ourselves that we do not know how to cope with. We close in on ourselves, we cease to believe in our way forward and our potentialities; our capacity for happiness and confidence wavers. Deep down, we ask ourselves: "What will become of me?" and in the confusion of our feelings we do not hear or do not manage to hear the clear reply that comes from God.

Jean Vanier, who founded the L'Arche Community that welcomes evangelically people who are seriously handicapped physically, has become an important prophetic voice in our own day. He shows clearly the importance of faith as a means of healing the wounds in our bodies and our souls. He has written:

> The essence of the Gospel is this: Judge no-one, even yourselves, condemn no-one not even yourselves, try to understand others and also yourselves. This is compassion. Compassion is not taking pity on someone, offering something sweet or some money. This too will often be necessary but it is not enough on its own. Compassion is to look at others (and ourselves) and help them to reveal themselves. Compassion is to show another that he or she is of value and that God dwells within that person. It is to help others to live to the utmost what they are capable of living.

In her anguish, Sarah tried to solve the problem of her sterility, but things did not work out too well.

> Now Sarah, Abraham's wife, bore him no children. She had an Egyptian maid whose name was Hagar; and Sarah said to Abraham, "Behold now, the Lord has prevented me from bearing children; go in to my maid; it may be that I shall obtain children by her." And Abraham hearkened to the voice of Sarah. So, after Abraham had dwelt ten years in the land of Canaan, Sarah, Abraham's wife, took Hagar the Egyptian, her maid, and gave her to Abraham her husband as a wife, And he went in to Hagar,

and she conceived; and when she saw that she had conceived, she looked with contempt on her mistress. And Sarah said to Abraham, "May the wrong done to me be on you! I gave my maid to your embrace, and when she saw that she had conceived, she looked upon me with contempt. May the Lord judge between you and me!" But Abraham said to Sarah, "Behold your maid is in your power; do to her as you please." Then Sarah dealt harshly with her, and she fled from her. (Gn 16:1-6)

Sarah was unsure of herself. She tried to find a solution outside herself, but the problem was right inside her. Her maltreatment and jealousy are a cry for help, fundamentally an interior upheaval. Sarah feels inadequate in front of Hagar. The competition between the slave girl and her mistress may well be imaginary, but Sarah lives it in reality. What is certain is that, inside herself, the wound remains open, perhaps made more serious by the failure of the attempt to heal it.

This knowledge of Sarah's lack of confidence in herself is important as it enables us to understand the hospitality scene described in the 18th chapter of Genesis, during which Sarah gets all flustered, denying that she had said what she did say. The cure for her is to follow the path of trust in God's promise:

The Lord appeared to Abraham by the oaks of Mamre, as he sat at the door of his tent in the heat of the day. He lifted up his eyes and looked, and behold, three men stood in front of him. When he saw them, he ran from the tent door to meet them, and bowed himself to the earth, and said, "My lord, if I have found favor in your sight, do not pass by your servant. Let a little water be brought, and wash your feet, and rest yourselves under the tree, while I fetch a morsel of bread, that you may refresh yourselves, and after that you may pass on – since there must surely be a purpose in your having come to your servant." So they said: "Do as you have said."

And Abraham hastened into the tent to Sarah, and said, "Make ready quickly three measures of fine meal, knead it, and make cakes." And Abraham ran to the herd, and took a calf, tender and good, and gave it to the servant, who hastened to prepare it. Then he took curds, and milk, and the calf which he had prepared, and set it before them; and he stood by them under the tree while they ate. They said to him, "Where is Sarah your wife?" And he said, "She is in the tent." One of them said, "I will surely return to you in the spring, and Sarah your wife shall have a son." And Sarah was listening at the tent door behind him. Now Abraham and Sarah were old, advanced in age; it had ceased to be with Sarah after the manner of women. So Sarah laughed to herself, saying, "After I have grown old, and my husband is old, shall I have this pleasure?" The Lord said to Abraham, "Why did Sarah laugh, and say, 'Shall I indeed bear a child, now that I am old?' Is anything too hard for the Lord? At the appointed time I will return to you, in the spring, and Sarah shall have a son." But Sarah denied, saying, "I did not laugh," for she was afraid. He said, "No, but you did laugh." (Gn 18:1-15)

Chapter 21 describes how Sarah conceived and gave birth to a son whom she named Isaac, which means literally "God smiled":

The Lord visited Sarah as he had said, and the Lord did to Sarah as he had promised And Sarah conceived, and bore Abraham a son in his old age at the time of which God had spoken to him. Abraham circumcised his son Isaac when he was eight days old, as God had commanded him. Abraham was a hundred years old when his son Isaac was born to him. And Sarah said: "God has made laughter for me; everyone who hears will laugh with me." And she said: "Who would have said to Abraham that Sarah would suckle children? Yet I have borne him a son in his old age." (Gn 21:1-7)

God smiles and makes us smile too. Let us trustingly open our hearts, with all their difficulties and wounds. Let us allow ourselves to be loved and guided by God. At the beginning of the Gospel, we hear the declaration that the Father makes about Jesus: "This is my beloved Son, in whom I am well pleased" (Mk 1:11). This is the deep meaning of the baptism of Jesus and of our own who were baptized in his name.

Our spiritual life begins there, in the certainty of God's dec-laration: "You are my beloved son, my beloved daughter, in whom I am well pleased."

When we reflect on the history of salvation, we see that there is a joy that is promised which is accomplished in time and in people's lives. As we sing in Psalm 125[6]:

> When the Lord delivered Sion from bondage,
> it seemed like a dream.
> Then was our mouth filled with laughter,
> on our lips there were songs.
> The heathens themselves said: "What marvels the
> Lord worked for them."
> What marvels the Lord worked for us!
> Indeed we were glad.
> Deliver us, O Lord, from our bondage like
> streams in dry land.
> Those who are sowing in tears
> will sing when they reap.
> They go out, they go out, full of tears,
> carrying seed for the sowing;
> they come back, they come back, full of song,
> carrying their sheaves.

6

❖

Our life is a landscape where God is seen

At the beginning of his encyclical, *Deus caritas est,* Pope Benedict XVI wrote: "God's love for us is fundamental for our lives,
and it raises important questions about who God is and who
we are." In fact, our lives are a landscape in which God is seen.
As each life is unique, there is something unique to which
each one of us can bear witness about God. The saints do this
magnificently. Anyone looking at our lives from outside may
well not perceive it, but we ourselves, who are living it with
God, perceive his mark on it, his passing, his loving kindness.
The love of God is a provident love, it is a love which enfolds
us in a way that is indescribable. According to St. John of the
Cross, "God is a sun suspended over souls, ready to communicate with them."

It is curious that in the Old Testament we find only two
direct references to the word "providence," both in the Book
of Wisdom. The Book of Wisdom may well be the most recent
of the books of the Old Testament (having been composed in
the second half of the first century before Christ), and was

already written in Greek, by a Jew with Hellenic culture. In it, the concept of providence occurs frequently. The first reference occurs in Wisdom 14:3 ("It is your providence, O Father, that steers its [the boat's] course, because you have given it a path in the sea"), and the second occurs in Wisdom 17:2, in a reference to lawless men who "are exiles from eternal providence."

Is it not strange that the concept of providence appears so rarely in the Old Testament? No, not if we bear in mind the originality of biblical thinking, with so little reference to abstract formulations, while so attentive to the description of facts, of reality. It is in the life of the People of God that the loving intervention of God is perceived. The certainty of this means that the Bible consists more of narratives and accounts of events than in philosophical reflections; it takes its descriptions of experiences and turns them into experience for those listening to the story. There can be no doubt that the experience of a providential God is at the heart of biblical faith. God did not abandon the world when he had finished creating it, but continues to operate in many ways within it, manifesting his concern, always close to our development over time. It would be sufficient, for example, to recall Psalm 103[4] which provides, at an extraordinary spiritual level, a meditation on the process of creation as a divine work in the here and now. At each moment of its existence, the world needs the support that comes to it from God, hopes for everything from God:

> Bless the Lord, my soul! Lord God, how great you are,
> Clothed in majesty and glory. (Ps 103[4]:1)

This same approach appears in other psalms. See, for example, Psalm 144[5]:15ff: "The eyes of all creatures look to you, and you give them their food in due time. You open wide your hand, grant the desires of all who live"; or Psalm 146[7]:7-8: "Sing to the Lord, giving thanks; sing psalms to our God with the harp. He covers the heavens with clouds; he prepares the rain for the earth, making mountains sprout with grass." But it appears also in the prophetic texts (Is 6:3; Ho 2:10) and the Wisdom books (Jb 9), so much so that it constitutes a kind of overall vision of biblical faith. Providence is experienced as the expression of a personal God and history becomes the decisive place in which he manifests himself.

The faith of Israel describes the almighty Lord of the world, in his Providence, with deep maternal feelings, seduced by displays of filial love, profoundly tender: "Is Ephraim my dear son? Is he my darling child? For as often as I speak of him, I do remember him still. Therefore my entrails yearn for him; I will surely have mercy on him, says the Lord" (Jr 31:20). "Entrails" or "womb," in Hebrew *rehamin*, denotes "the most intimate part" of one's being, the source of that ever enduring love. It is here that Providence is rooted: it is the expression of a love that cannot but love at every moment, in every gesture. In the biblical tradition, the theological treatment of Providence is like a photographic lens which brings the loving face of God close to us.

This movement of coming close can be well understood and prayed in the word of Psalm 64[5]:

> To you our praise is due in Sion, O God.
> To you we pay our vows,

you who hear our prayer.
To you all flesh will come with its burden of sin.
Too heavy for us, our offences,
but you wipe them away.
Blessed he whom you choose and call
to dwell in your courts.
We are filled with the blessings of your house,
of your holy temple.
You keep your pledge with wonders,
O God our Savior,
the hope of all the earth
and of far distant isles.
You uphold the mountains with your strength,
You are girded with power.
You still the roaring of the seas,
the roaring of their waves
and the tumult of the peoples.
The ends of the earth stand in awe
at the sight of your wonders.
The lands of sunrise and sunset
you fill with your joy.
You care for the earth, give it water,
you fill it with riches.
Your river in heaven brims over
to provide its grain.
And thus you provide for the earth;
you drench it with furrows,
you level it, soften it with showers,
you bless its growth.

You crown the year with your goodness.
Abundance flows in your steps,
in the pastures of the wilderness it flows.
The hills are girded with joy,
the meadows covered with flocks,
the valleys are decked with wheat.
They sing for joy, yes, they sing.

1. The composition begins by situating us in the Temple, the space where God reveals his salvific action (vv. 2-5) on behalf of the believing community.

2. After praising the divine activity in the Temple, it moves on to praise God's activity in the world; from the sacred microcosm it moves out to the cosmos transfigured by the presence of the One who is all-powerful. God is described, in grandiose terms, as a cosmic architect according to the classic model that is called for above all by the Wisdom literature (vv. 7-9).

3. There follows a third change of register. In a lovely way, God is then presented as a peasant in the rural Palestinian countryside, a *pater familias* who works the land, reaps the wheat and toils to feed his family (vv. 10-14). From one image to the other (from the epic one to begin with to this second intimate and bucolic image, portraying in delightful miniature the day-to-day life of the fields), only a very superficial reading would detect any form of toning down or diminishing the power of the metaphor. In fact, it is quite the opposite. In a way, the

entire psalm moves towards this lovely simple final scene where it is clear that the psalmist has allowed himself to be captivated by the tenderness of God.

We can say that the biblical theology of Providence consists in the expression of repeated wonder and astonishment for the ways in which God is present throughout history. God is a peasant (Psalm 64[5]) or a mother who, in this way, expresses her love for her child: "I have carved you on the palm of my hand" (Is 49:16), or a husband who, through love, ignores the adulterous past of his bride (Ho 1-3). "God is a man of war" (Ex 15:3) or he is peace (Nb 6:26). His watchfulness is as wide as the extended wings of an eagle (Ex 19:4). He cherishes the fruit of the womb and the fruits of the earth. He blesses the wheat and the new wine. He makes both fields and flocks flourish (Dt 7:13). He is the Lord of the celebration (Dt 16:16) and the spectator of the dance (2 S 6:16), but he also "turns his ear" in a day of trouble and wipes the tears from our eyes (Ps 114[116]). "Fortress" (Ps 61[2]:7): "a sun, a shield" (Ps 83[4]:12); "Rock" (Ps 88[9]:27): "guard" and "shade" (Ps 120[1]:5): all these descriptions constitute an existential and committed murmuring of the litany that is always with us and that can be extended infinitely: God's Providence.

In Jesus' preaching, providence coincides with the exercise of the fatherhood of God: "Your heavenly Father knows that you need these things" (Mt 6:32): it is this certainty of the providential action of God which enables Jesus to say: "Do not be anxious about your life," rather "seek first the kingdom of God and his justice" (Mt 6:25, 33). In the path that Jesus maps out for us, God's help is certain whatever happens because, like the Shepherd of the lost sheep, "it is not the will of my Father who is in heaven that one of these little ones should perish" (Mt 18:14). Hence it is that, at a time of persecution, "when they deliver you up, do not be anxious how you are to speak or what you are to say; for what you are to say will be given to you in that hour" (Mt 10:19) or, if it comes to having to face martyrdom: "Do not fear those who kill the body but cannot kill the soul... for even the hairs of your head are all numbered" (Mt 10:28, 30).

In the passage from Matthew 7:9-11, the emphasis on Providence is particularly striking: "If you then, who are evil, know how to give good gifts to your children, how much more will your Father who is in heaven give good things to those who ask him!" (Mt 7:11). Jesus urges us to trust absolutely in God as one trusts in the tender love of a father who lets the sun of his tenderness and his loving care shine on each and every one (Mt 5:45).

The providential love of God is clearly revealed in the life and destiny of Jesus himself. As St. Paul has written: "Neither death, nor life, nor angels, nor principalities, nor things present, nor things to come, nor powers, nor height, nor depth, nor anything else in all creation, will be able to separate us from the love of God in Christ Jesus our Lord" (Rm 8:38-39). Here we are perhaps touching the most characteristic aspect of the New Testament faith in Providence: that which regards Providence not merely as a manifestation of God in time, but as the ultimate purpose of history itself. The sense of history is in the love of God. As Pope Benedict XVI has written: "It could hardly be otherwise since its promise looks towards its definitive goal: love looks to the eternal" (*Deus caritas est,* 6).

It is clear that Providence must not be confused with "providentialism." Jesus himself has warned us against this temptation: "Then the devil took him to the holy city and set him on the pinnacle of the temple, and said to him, 'If you are the Son of God, throw yourself down, for it is written: *He will give his angels charge of you; on their hands they will bear you up lest you strike your foot against a stone.'* Jesus said to him, 'Again it is written, *You shall not tempt the Lord your God'*" (Mt 4:5-7). Providence does not cancel out the condition of human freedom. On the contrary, it appears as an expression of God's fidelity to the Covenant. God is faithful. In our own history and in the history of the world, Providence appears as the Covenant of Love, in which we really can have confidence: "And I tell you, ask, and it will be given you; seek, and you will find; knock and it will be opened to you. For everyone who asks receives; and he who seeks finds, and to him who knocks it will be opened" (Lk 11:9-10).

We know very well who it is in whom we have placed our trust. And so we can pray, in the words that conclude a poem by Sophia de Mello Breyner Andresen:

> All I know is that I walk
> As one who knows that he/she is being watched,
>   is loved and known
> And so in everything I do
> I combine solemnity with risk.

7

❖

Show us the Father

Sometimes, in order to get a better idea of this whole question
of managing to pray, it may be worth looking at the words
of one of our contemporaries who describes precisely the opposite experience, a radical difficulty in relation to the experience of praying. I am quoting from the first few pages of an
autobiographical text by the Italian writer Erri de Luca. The
text is entitled *Nocciolo d'oliva,* and in it the author writes:

> Being an assiduous reader of Sacred Scripture, I
> work my way through the ancient Hebrew of the
> early histories, of the prophets, and of the psalms
> that have been gathered together in the Old Testa-
> ment. This daily practice has not made a believer
> of me. For me, the experience of being an outsider
> is the result of two obstacles. The first is prayer,
> this power and possibility of the believer to express
> him- or her- self, to address God as "Thou" or "You."
> Whoever it was who expressed for the first time the
> first prayer cannot have invented it, but can only

have reacted to a call with a reply. [For my part] I do not know how to do it. I do not know how to address myself to Him. [...] I speak about God in the third person, I read about Him, I hear Him spoken of and I perceive others living in Him. [However] in spite of all this, I remain a person who speaks about God in the third person. My foot trips every day over this stone of prayer; it cannot get past it because prayer is the door post. The other obstacle is forgiveness. I do not know how to forgive and I cannot allow myself to be forgiven. [...] There is, in my life, a boundary line of the unpardonable, of the "never can be forgiven." I cannot allow myself to be forgiven. I do not know how to forgive the things I have done. These are the stones I trip over, and it is because of them that I remain outside the community of Christians.

If we think about prayer, there are limits and stones to trip over in all our lives. A person is only able to long for God, is only capable of entering into a relationship with God because it is God who leans down benevolently towards that person. It is by believing that this is so that believers present themselves before God, and not because they feel emboldened by their own merits or gifts. The impressive collection of metaphors that we find in Sacred Scripture is a way of expressing this fundamental trust that makes it possible for prayer to be a "face to face between man and God." We draw close to God because God draws close to us. And God is father and

mother, shepherd and king. God is strong and mysterious like
the gentle breeze. God dwells in the inner sanctuary of the
temple or comes to embrace us in the darkness of the journey,
as the patriarch Jacob discovered in his struggle with the angel which, as we see in the magnificent picture by Delacroix
[in the Church of Saint-Sulpice in Paris] seems more a dance
than a wrestling match.... The very Spirit of God unites itself
with our own spirit in order to overcome our weakness and
bring us close to Him. "Likewise the Spirit helps us in our
weakness; for we do not know how to pray as we ought, but
the Spirit himself intercedes for us with sighs too deep for
words" (Rm 8:26).

But the closeness of God which we experience does not
do away with, nor can it do away with, the sensation of distance which the believer perceives in relation to God, because
God is infinitely Other. For this reason, prayer is also a cry
("My soul is yearning for you, my God. My soul is thirsting for
God, the God of my life" Ps 41[2]:2-3), an appeal, a petition,
a suggestion of greater intimacy in some ways like the art of
lovemaking, as indeed we are reminded in the Song of Songs:
"Draw me after you. Let us make haste! The king has brought
me into his chambers" (Sg 1:4).

Underlying all prayer is the pair of opposites – closeness/
distance – which is experienced in the relationship of human
beings with God. A distance maintained, because God is
God. But it is also a closeness that is willed because God is
love. Pope Benedict XVI has explained this as follows: "On
the one hand we find ourselves before a strictly metaphysical
image of God: God is the absolute and ultimate source of

all being; but this universal principle of creation – the *Logos*, primordial reason – is at the same time a lover with all the passion of a true love" (*Deus caritas est,* 10).

For us Christians, Jesus overcomes the distance between earth and heaven. "He who sees me sees him who sent me" (Jn 12:45). As Kierkegaard has said, the Christian is someone who, through the mediation of Christ, feels himself continually in the presence of God. This philosopher criticized the Christianity of his own day which, according to him, was too much wrapped up in philosophical concepts, and was forgetting this other, most astonishing, thing: to exist is to exist in Christ, in the presence of God. We ourselves also easily get lost in abstractions. Christ gives us the "daring" to commit ourselves in trusting prayer to the Father. The Roman Missal uses the expression: "audemus dicere" (we dare to say), and this is what it is all about.

The New Testament contains two versions of the prayer that Jesus taught to his disciples: in St. Matthew (6:9-15) and St. Luke (11:1-4). There are small differences between the two versions, as Luke's is more concise, but basically they are identical. Let us look at the text from the Gospel of St. Matthew:

> Our Father who art in heaven
> Hallowed be thy name
> Thy kingdom come,
> Thy will be done,
> On earth as it is in heaven.
> Give us this day our daily bread,
> And forgive us our debts,
> As we have forgiven our debtors;

And lead us not into temptation,
But deliver us from evil.

Everything in the prayer of the *Our Father*, whether as regards the circumstances relating to its transmission, or as regards the basic synthesis of its composition, shows that Jesus intended to present a model. In the Jewish tradition to which, as a matter of history, Jesus himself belonged, there are a number of praying traditions and a rich collection of prayer formulas. But Jesus does something different: not only does he explain how to pray, but he hands on his teaching about prayer beginning with an eloquent command: "Pray like this." In this way, he clearly marks out a pathway to prayer.

Now, as we begin to examine the prayer of Jesus, we perceive that it all turns on the vocative form with which the prayer begins: "Our Father" (in Matthew's version) or quite simply "Father" as in that of St. Luke. It is true that there follow, after the Name, references to the Will and the Kingdom, but we continue to be gathered around the discovery of the Father. Instead of asking to be granted this or that, or pleading for the satisfaction of some lack that we feel, what the Father is being asked is that he be in fact our Father. The one to whom the prayer is addressed, the Person we are addressing, emerges as the object of our petition.

Another significant aspect is that if we arrange this prayer rhetorically, if we look closely at the way in which the phrases follow one another, we perceive the following: the first word is "Father" and the last word is "Evil." This being so, the pattern of the text is seen to be invested with an important meaning, when it shows us that evil appears at the furthermost point opposed to the Father, i.e. that evil is the anti-Father. It is essential for us to understand this. The risk of a confrontation with evil is a possibility that can occur in the existence of anyone. Evil crosses our path, may even pierce us at times, but the prayer which Jesus gives us asks for light to enable us not to be deceived in the Father, in other words, that we will not allow ourselves to become attached to evil, dependent on it, as if it could be a substitute for the real Father. We pray so that we can know how to choose the Father at all times and not any of the counterfeits that at times seek to obscure or blot out in us the solid framework of his Presence.

A prayer which describes fatherhood so intimately is at the heart of the identity of the praying subject. It is not a mere form of words, but the expression of one's self, a relational choreography, an awareness of the being that is coming into being. Let us listen to Emanuel Levinas:

> My son is not something I have produced. Moreover, he does not belong to me. Neither the category of power or of wisdom describes my relationship with my son. The fertility of the "I" is neither cause nor domination. I do not possess my son, I am my son. Fatherhood is a relationship with another who, though another being, is an extension of myself. The son is not myself; nevertheless I am my son.

Thinking about the *Our Father,* we can say that the purpose of the prayer is to place us in the Father, inscribe us in his heart: I am in the Father, I exist in the Father. The chief

Christian prayer is not a list of petitions but the expression of a trusting relationship. This is the originality of Jesus. The direct appeal to the Father is very unusual in the Jewish tradition. And it is seen to be even more significant when, in the brief space of such a sober prayer as the *Our Father*, Jesus chooses voluntarily to bring the praying heart back to its essence: the Father. As François Genuyt has written: This concentration culminates in a "search which is not only addressed to the Father, but is a search for the Father." We can say with the disciple Philip: "Show us the Father, and we shall be satisfied" (Jn 14:8). Or with the Brazilian poetess Adelia Prado: "My God puts his hand in mine, heals me of my ambition. O my God, my father, my father."

The discovery that Simone Weil made of the *Our Father* occupies one of the most intense pages of her spiritual autobiography. It all begins with a desire, which she confided in her spiritual counselor, Father Perrin. Throughout the year 1941, she expressed the need she felt to return to an activity of her teenage summers; to be in direct contact with the earth, contributing to the work of producing food. It is not a scheme that is easy to explain, this desire to become a country girl, when her closest friends were all trying to convince her that what she should be doing was to concentrate on the branches of knowledge in which she had specialized: philosophy, poetry, writing and speaking. During those months, she multiplied herself in letters and in explanations in order to back up her contention that the purification of the agricultural effort gave her an energy that she had found nowhere else. It was then, at the suggestion of Father Perrin, that she contacted Gustave

Thibon, who was to be so important in making known the thought of the young philosopher. Simone was to appear at his fifth farm, in Saint-Marcel-d'Ardèche, at the beginning of August 1941, where she was to remain for two months. She refused to stay in the main farmhouse and went to live on her own in a rickety old shed with few amenities, to the dismay of her hosts. But Gustave Thibon has described how, on one of the early days of her stay, when he did not quite know what to think of that young lady, he saw Simone leaning out of a tree and contemplating the valley. Later, he reported: "I saw her eyes slowly emerge from what she had been looking at; the intensity and purity of her look were such that I felt that she was contemplating interior depths as well as the splendid view that lay before her. The beauty of her soul corresponded to the majesty of the panorama." It was the sealing of a great friendship. It was there that Simone Weil discovered the *Our Father,* perhaps by an unusual route. She herself wrote as follows:

> Last summer, doing Greek with T- (Thibon), I went through the *Our Father* word for word in Greek. We promised each other to learn it by heart. I do not think he ever did so, and I did not do much more, at that point. But some weeks later, as I was turning over the pages of the Gospel, I said to myself that since I had promised to do this thing and it was good, I ought to do it. I did it. The infinite sweetness of this Greek text so took hold of me that for several days I could not stop myself from saying it over all the time. A week afterward I began the

vine harvest. I recited the *Our Father* in Greek every day before work, and I repeated it very often in the vineyard. Since that time I have made a practice of saying it through once each morning with absolute attention. If during the recitation my attention wanders or goes to sleep in the minutest degree, I begin again until I have succeeded in going through it once with absolutely pure attention.

The effect of this practice is extraordinary and surprises me every time, for, although I experience it each day, it exceeds my expectation at each repetition. At times the very first words tear my thoughts from my body and transport it to a place outside space where there is neither perspective nor point of view. The infinity of the ordinary expanses of perception is replaced by an infinity to the second or sometimes the third degree. At the same time, filling every part of this infinity of infinity, there is silence, a silence which is not an absence of sound but which is the object of a positive sensation, more positive than that of sound. Noises, if there are any, only reach me after crossing this silence. Sometimes, also, during this recitation or at other moments, Christ is present with me in person, but his presence is infinitely more real, more moving, more clear than on that first occasion when he took possession of me.[2]

---

[2] Simone Weil, Letter to Fr. Perrin, in *Waiting on God*.

For Simone, the *Our Father* "is to prayer as Christ is to humanity" and "it is impossible to say it, once you are doing so and you are giving to each word your full attention, without a change, perhaps infinitesimal but real taking place in one's soul." Simone Weil was concerned about the effectiveness of the praying word in the soul, that is, its sharp ability to transform us spiritually and existentially. She is not concerned with the historical or critical commentary, but with the radiance, the glow, the real shock, the affective and effective conversion which the prayer of Jesus in ourselves arouses. There is a moment in which what counts are not the words but the fact of being there in relationship: "Lord, show us the Father, and we shall be satisfied" (Jn 14:8).

8

❖

Coming to terms with beauty

"What is capable of restoring enthusiasm and confidence, what can encourage the human spirit to rediscover its path, to raise its eyes to the horizon, to dream of a life worthy of its vocation if not beauty?" This serious and existentially decisive question was asked by Pope Benedict XVI in the Sistine Chapel in November 2009, during his historic meeting with artists. The very nature of the question makes it clear that it is not addressed solely to artists of all kinds; rather, it is a challenge addressed to each one of us. In fact, the question of beauty is absolutely central to Christian experience, to, I repeat, everyday Christian experience, and it is urgent that we should feel the need to become reconciled with beauty.

Nowadays it may well astonish us to discover that one of the topics discussed by the Fathers of the Church was whether or not Christ was beautiful. It is by no means the secondary or futile question that it might appear to be at first sight. In fact, the Liturgy itself continues to feed this debate. For example, it is the Liturgy that applies Psalm 44[5] to Jesus:

My heart overflows with noble words.
To the king I must speak the song I have made;
my tongue as nimble as the pen of a scribe.

You are the fairest of the children of men
and graciousness is poured upon your lips:
because God has blessed you for evermore.

It is a wedding psalm, which begins with a description of the beauty of the king, his courage and valor and his noble mission, followed by a description of the exaltation of the bride:

Listen, O Daughter, give ear to my words:
Forget your own people and your father's house.
So will the king desire your beauty.
He is your lord, pay homage to him.

Christian tradition has interpreted this psalm as a prefiguring of the nuptial relationship between Christ and the Church. In his "The Beauty and the Truth of Christ," the then Cardinal Joseph Ratzinger wrote that the Church "recognizes Christ as the fairest of men, the grace poured upon his lips points to the inner beauty of his words, the glory of his proclamation. So it is not merely the external beauty of the Redeemer's appearance that is glorified: rather, the beauty of Truth appears in him, the beauty of God himself who draws us to himself and at the same time captures us with the wound of Love, the holy passion that enables us to go forth together, with and in the Church his Bride, to meet the Love who calls us."

Beauty, and the beauty of Christ in particular, captures our heart, wounds us intimately, opens us to revelation, works in such a way that we cease to belong to ourselves, forces us to relativize what we were, and frequently to forget our country of origin and our father's house, draws us to itself. It is this that the Church prays for in Psalm 44[5].

But while the Liturgy uses the psalm frequently, it also deems indispensable the light that is shed on the mystery of Christ by the drama of the Suffering Servant described so vividly in Isaiah 53:1-4:

> Who has believed what we have heard;
> and to whom has the arm of the Lord been revealed?
> For he grew up before him like a young plant,
> and like a root out of dry ground;
> he had no form or comeliness that we should look
>   at him,
> and no beauty that we should desire him.
> He was despised and rejected by men;
> a man of sorrows and acquainted with grief;
> and as one from whom men hid their faces
> he was despised, and we esteemed him not.
> Surely he has borne our griefs and carried our sorrows:
> yet we esteemed him stricken, smitten by God
>   and afflicted.

How, then, are we to reconcile spiritually the two texts? In the first one, Christ is "the fairest of the children of men," while in the other he appears completely disfigured, with "no form or comeliness that we should look on him." Pilate, perhaps in an attempt to evoke some compassion for him, presented him to the crowd as "the Man": "Behold the Man" (Jn 19:5). I quote again from Cardinal Ratzinger:

> Implicit here is the more radical question of whether beauty is true or whether it is not ugliness that leads us to the deepest truth of reality. Whoever believes in God, in the God who manifested himself precisely in the altered appearance of Christ crucified as love to the end (Jn 13:1), knows that beauty is truth and truth beauty; but in the suffering Christ he also learns that the beauty of truth also embraces offence, pain, and even the dark mystery of death, and that this can only be found in accepting suffering, not in ignoring it.

In fact, there is no beauty which is not somehow stitched together by the mystery of the cross, which does not place us, like Mary and John, at the foot of the cross.

Why is it that reconciliation with the beauty of Christ is so decisive in the maturing of a spiritual journey? Without beauty, a Christian's experience remains incomplete. We know very well the dangers inherent in an exclusively sociological Christianity, one that functions only between convictions and praxis. History tells us of geologists who, in their investigations, discovered a lake at the top of very high mountains, and in this lake there were stones which had been there for hundreds of years. However, when they split them in order to study their morphological properties, they discovered to their amazement that inside they were dry. In the same way, without the attractive beauty of Christ, Christianity is dry, functional, bureaucratic, ritualistic, an outward bath of conventions to which our hearts remain impervious. But our heart is called to be wounded by the paschal beauty of Christ and the infinite Love that he reveals. Our vocation is this wound of love, this plunging into, this soaking ourselves to the marrow of our bones in the love of God, this living of a real belonging which the longing for God sets fire to in our lives, this experiencing a thrill of God which goes on for years ("I slept, but my heart was awake" Sg 5:2), this passion which does not discourage in view of the absolute of God and of God alone, this manifestation of Love which challenges, transfigures and transcends us day by day, this inexplicable light of God which both knocks us down and raises us up on our way to Damascus.

Plato explained the impact of beauty on us as follows and his explanation is very helpful because to be wounded by beauty is, above all, an anthropological experience. "When one looks upon beauty, a reaction like shuddering comes over one, with sweat and unwonted heat. For as the effluence of beauty enters through one's eyes, one's essence is warmed and watered." Is this not what occurred within the two disciples on the way to Emmaus: "Did not our hearts burn within us while he talked to us on the road, while he opened to us the Scriptures?" (Lk 23:32). The Christian may be defined as someone who has been "wounded" by the singular beauty of Jesus. And this "wound" evokes within us a desire, a wish, an attraction, a readiness to follow.

The mysterious struggle of Jacob with God (Gn 32:25-32) represents, paradigmatically, the way in which the inrush of the divine is that of a mightier beauty which overcomes us, a beauty that is irresistible, but which remains inexpressible:

And Jacob was left alone, and a man wrestled with him until the breaking of the day. When the man saw that he did not prevail against Jacob, he touched the hollow of his thigh; and Jacob's thigh was put out of joint as he wrestled with him. Then he said: "Let me go, for the day is breaking." But Jacob said, "I will not let you go, unless you bless me." And he said to him, "What is your name?" And he said, "Jacob." Then he said, "Your name shall no more be called Jacob, but Israel, for you have striven with God and with men and have prevailed." Then Jacob asked him, "Tell me, I pray, your name." But he said, "Why is it that you ask my name?" And there he blessed him. So Jacob called the place Penuel, saying, "For I have seen God face to face, and yet my life is preserved." The sun was beginning to rise as he passed Penuel, limping because of his thigh.

"The sun was beginning to rise." The encounter with Beauty is so decisive that there is a before and an after, it is a new stage which is beginning in our lives. And it is intriguing to reflect on the fact that Jacob is left limping as a result of his struggle with the angel. He has been wounded because the Beauty of God is wounding, there is nothing superficial about it. The Beauty of God summons men and women to their final destination, reveals to them the real greatness of truth. In his *Life in Christ,* the important Byzantine theologian, Nicholas Cabasilas (14ᵗʰ century) wrote as follows: "It is the Bridegroom who has smitten us with this longing. It is he who has sent a ray of his beauty into our eyes. While the greatness of the wound already shows that the arrow has struck home, the longing indicates who has inflicted the wound" [cf. *The Life in Christ,* Book II, §15].

In fact, the other two transcendentals, Truth and Goodness, have no capacity to attract people unless they have been touched by "something which fascinates," as Plotinus wrote. It is Beauty that attracts, draws the heart, takes hold and transforms. For this reason, we must move beyond the silence to which it had been relegated by a certain rationalistic outlook, even with Christian theology and spirituality. Let us come to terms with Beauty, let us allow ourselves to be transformed interiorly by it. Cardinal Ratzinger goes on to tell us:

> Being struck and overcome by the beauty of Christ is more real, more profound knowledge than mere rational deduction. Of course we must not underrate the importance of theological reflection, of exact and precise theological thought; it remains absolutely necessary. But to move from here to disdain or to reject the impact produced by the response of the heart in the encounter with beauty as a true form of knowledge would impoverish us and dry up our faith and our theology. We must rediscover this form of knowledge; it is a pressing need of our time.

As it developed over time, Christian experience became the seedbed for some astonishing expressions of beauty: religious architecture, from Michelangelo to Gaudi; the luminous reflections left to us by the mystics (think only of Hildegard of Bingen or St. John of the Cross); the vast range of paintings and icons which reproduce the incommensurable line by line (the crowds that flock there day after day clearly show that the Sistine Chapel thrills everyone); musical compositions ringing like inventories with the needs and longings of the soul, or like a momentary flash of insight; immense dictionaries describing the natural and the supernatural; signs and symbols, the laboratory of languages which are forever growing richer. But all these expressions can become merely equivocal, because Beauty is not a patrimony that the Church owned or owns or simply administers. Beauty belongs to the revelation of the Church itself, to its supernatural identity. This is the "great mystery" that is spoken of in the Letter to the Ephesians (5:25-26): "Christ loved the Church and gave himself up for her, that he might sanctify her, having cleansed her ... that he might present the Church in splendor, without spot or wrinkle." The Church in Christ, in the mystery of her nature and her mission, is the dawning of the vision, it is this historic and, from God's point of view, infinite rapture. In a veiled but tremendously effective way, it constitutes the expression and drama of divine wisdom. This was how Dionysius the Areopagite wrote, citing the example of St. Paul:

> Paul the Sublime, having felt the spur of the divine
> Eros and become a sharer in its ecstatic power, cried

out: "I live, but it is no longer I who live, but Christ who lives in me" [Gal 2:20]. He speaks, then, like a true lover, like someone who, as he himself says, is beside himself and lives ecstatically in God (2 Cor 5:15) to such an extent that he no longer lives his own life but that of the beloved, like someone who is filled with passionate love.

The key declaration, so often commented on, made by Jesus in John's Gospel (10:11), and that we are accustomed to seeing translated all over the place as "I am the good shepherd," in fact has another possible meaning. It can be translated as "I am the beautiful shepherd." During his apostolic visit to Portugal, Benedict XVI left us this challenge: "Produce beautiful things, but above all make your lives places of beauty." Let us allow ourselves to be touched, enchanted, fall in love with, and be wounded by the Beauty which God reveals in Jesus.

9

❖

Praying until we can pray no more

Throughout his life, at every moment in his life, Jesus prayed. Take, for example, the evidence we find for this in the Gospel of St. Luke. It was "when Jesus was praying" that the Spirit descended on him at his baptism (3:21): "You are my beloved Son; with you I am well pleased." Before he chose the twelve apostles, he spent the entire night in prayer to God (6:12). The question that elicited Peter's confession of faith was put to the disciples "one day when he was praying" (9:18). Moreover, when one of his disciples asked him to teach them, too, how to pray, it was because this disciple saw the Lord himself praying (11:1). Christ prayed so that Peter's faith would not fail (22:32) and, when nailed to the cross, he prayed to the Father: "Father, forgive them, for they do not know what they are doing" (23:46), and also for himself: "Father, into your hands I commend my spirit" (23:76).

For Jesus, prayer was not merely a part of his life, it *was* his life. At every moment, he lived his existence in the presence of God, his Father. Jesus hid nothing from the Father.

His joys and sorrows, his hopes and his nights were always shared with the Father.

Christian prayer is not a journey to the depths of one's self. It is not an exercise in introspection. It is not a diagnosis of our external or inner thoughts and feelings. Christian prayer is being and standing in the presence of God, placing oneself completely and continuously in his presence, paying watchful attention to the One who summons us to an unbroken dialogue. It is not to offer to God some thoughts, but to commit to him all our thoughts, everything that we are and experience.

Prayer entails a change of attitude, because true prayer detaches us from ourselves – from our worries and concerns, from our selfish and far from pure wishes – and turns us towards God in such a way that the only thing we begin to wish for is the will of God, the gift of his eye upon us who, as St. Augustine used to say, "is nearer to us than we are to ourselves." This is expressed very well in Blessed Charles de Foucauld's *Prayer of Abandonment:*

Father,
I abandon myself into your hands;
do with me what you will.
Whatever you may do, I thank you:
I am ready for all, I accept all.

Let only your will be done in me,
and in all your creatures –
I wish no more than this, O Lord.

Into your hands I commend my soul:
I offer it to you with all the love of my heart,
for I love you, Lord, and so need to give myself,
to surrender myself into your hands without reserve,
and with boundless confidence, for you are my Father.

How much time should we spend in prayer? It is essential for there to be key moments in this daily journey of self-abandonment and, realistically speaking, we absolutely must set aside a portion of the day for God and God alone. But let us not deceive ourselves: prayer cannot be just one compartment of my day, a little niche which I fill with pious thoughts and formulas. Christian prayer is the prayer that is said as we follow in Jesus' footsteps and, this being so, to pray is to live with all our strength and all our reality in the presence of God. We need to get away from an egocentric concept of prayer and develop instead a theocentric one, founded affectively and effectively on God. When we look steadily at Jesus, our eyes and our heart learn, in the grace of the Holy Spirit, the way to the Father. The whole Being of Jesus is an abiding intimacy and revelation of the Father. "No one has seen the Father except him who is from God; he has seen the Father" (Jn 6:46).

How much time should we spend in prayer? We must begin to feel inside ourselves that we are praying all the time. There is perhaps no other simpler or more vibrant way to understand the nature of the prayer of Jesus. What a marvelous and necessary lesson in prayer we are given in that Russian classic of Christian spirituality entitled: *The Way of a Pilgrim*, which begins as follows:

By the grace of God I am a Christian, by my actions a great sinner and by calling a homeless wanderer of the humblest birth who roams from place to place. My worldly goods are a knapsack with some dried bread in it on my back, and in my breast-pocket a Bible. And that is all. On the 24th Sunday after Pentecost I went to church to say my prayers during the Liturgy. The First Epistle of Saint Paul to the Thessalonians was being read and among other words I heard these: *"Pray without ceasing"* (1 Th 5:17). It was this text, more than any other, which forced itself upon my mind, and I began to think how it was possible to pray without ceasing since a man has to concern himself with other things also in order to make a living.

The truth is that our conversion to unceasing prayer is far from easy. We experience an inexplicable resistance to the idea of living as vulnerable beings, poor and defenseless before God. Adam and Eve were not the only ones who went and hid when they heard the Lord God walking in the garden (Gn 3:8). Naturally, we open ourselves to loving God and adoring him, but we also wish to keep part of our spiritual lives for ourselves. As a result we fall frequently into the temptation of choosing very carefully the thoughts that we want to have in our minds in our colloquies with God. Whether through fear or a feeling of insecurity, we easily think of prayer as being unduly introspective and often hide from God (can we really hide from him?) the very things in ourselves which most need his transforming and calming action.

The Russian pilgrim's journey was a long one, and our own journey will be a long one too. However, with the help of the praying community, he really does reach the point at which prayer becomes the active presence of the Spirit of God, leading our lives by the hand.

Let us recall some of the key words and phrases that constituted stepping stones along the Russian pilgrim's journey which, when all is said and done, is the journey of every true Christian:

1. "The Apostle says, *Pray without ceasing* (1 Th 5:17), that is, he teaches us to have the remembrance of God in all times and places and circumstances. If you are making something you must call to mind the Creator of all things; if you see the light, remember the Giver of it; if you see the heavens and the earth and the sea and all that is in them, wonder and praise the Maker of them. If you put on your clothes recall Whose gift they are and thank Him Who provides for your life. In short, let every action be a cause of your remembering and praising God, and lo! you will be praying without ceasing and therein your soul will always rejoice."

2. "Ceaseless interior prayer is a continual yearning of the human spirit towards God. To succeed in this consoling exercise we must ask God to teach us to pray without ceasing. Pray more, and pray more fervently. It is prayer itself that will reveal to you how it can be achieved unceasingly, but it will take some time."

3. "Thank God, my dear brother, for having revealed to you this unappeasable desire for unceasing interior prayer. Recognize in it the call of God, and calm yourself. Rest assured that what has hitherto been accomplished in you is the testing of the harmony of your own will with the voice of God. It has been granted to you to understand that the heavenly light of unceasing interior prayer is attained neither by the wisdom of this world, nor by the mere outward desire for knowledge, but that, on the contrary, it is found in poverty of spirit and in active experience in simplicity of heart."

4. "Sit down alone and in silence. Lower your head, shut your eyes, breathe out gently and imagine yourself looking into your own heart. Carry your mind, that is, your thoughts, from your head to your heart. As you breathe out, say: 'Lord Jesus Christ, have mercy on me.' Say it moving your lips gently or simply say it in your mind. Try to put all other thoughts aside. Be calm and repeat the process very frequently."

5. "The continuous interior Prayer of Jesus is a constant uninterrupted calling upon the divine name of Jesus with the lips, in spirit, in the heart, while forming a mental picture of his constant presence and imploring his grace during every occupation and in all places even during sleep. The appeal is couched in these terms: 'Lord Jesus Christ, have mercy on me.' After no great lapse of time, I had the feeling that the Prayer had, so to speak, by its own action, passed from my lips to my heart. That is to

say, it seemed as though my heart in its ordinary beating began to say the Prayer within each beat. Thus, for example, *one* Lord *two* Jesus *three* Christ, and so on. I gave up saying the prayer with my lips. I simply listened carefully to what my heart was saying."

Jesus is the true Master of Christian prayer, both because his own prayer was the model of all prayer and because it is he who teaches us to pray. The parable of Jesus that we find in Luke 18:9-14 is an important lesson in prayer.

> Two men went up into the temple to pray, one a Pharisee and the other a tax collector. The Pharisee stood and prayed thus with himself. "God, I thank you that I am not like other men, extortionists, unjust, adulterers, or even like this tax collector. I fast twice a week; I give tithes of all that I get." But the tax collector, standing far off, would not even lift up his eyes to heaven, but beat his breast, saying, "God, be merciful to me the sinner!" I tell you, this man went down to his house justified rather than the other; for everyone who exalts himself will be humbled, but he who humbles himself will be exalted.

We can pray with the Pharisee. The opening vocative "O God" confers a solemn and rhetorical tone to his prayer. His prayer is a self-referential one: "I," "I," "I" is repeated over and over again. His praise is based on the difference that he perceives between himself and others, which are this, that and the other: robbers, adulterers, unjust, who are above all like that tax collector standing behind him in the temple. He is a good practicing Pharisee reflecting on himself, dazzled by his good works which, in his prayer, are neither penitential nor suppliant in character.

While the Pharisee makes use of the space without undue concern or anxiety (he simply stands there and talks, talks a lot), the tax collector is aware of what is near to him and what is far away, of what is high and low, body and word: he feels "far off," he does not dare to raise his eyes and beats his breast as he utters a few words. He realizes what it is that keeps him at a distance. He does not move horizontally but vertically. He does not pretend to have a closeness that does not exist. Instead, he shows himself as he is to God. When, in his prayer, he describes himself as a "sinner," he is not using a mere figure of speech, he is stating an existential truth which is vibrantly borne out by the symbolic intensity of his bodily posture.

A number of writers have stated that the tax collector's gesture in striking his breast is to be interpreted as a sign of contrition. The most common meaning of this gesture in the world of that time was that of an intense emotion, evoked by a disappointment of some kind or by a desperate situation, combined also with a feeling of regret. However, his anxiety is not total: from the bitter depth of his night he calls out to God and he prays: "O God, have mercy on me, the sinner." This passage is the only one in the Gospel in which the "sinner" uses the definite article to identify himself "the sinner." This does not mean that the tax collector is the greatest sinner on the face of the earth, but that is what he feels he is as he stands before God.

The spiritual significance of the turning point in the parable is this attitude of the tax collector, in marked contrast with that of the Pharisee. He directs towards God his entire life, his hang-ups, his tears, his despair. He makes himself utterly dependent on God. Let God do what he will. Let God have mercy. To pray is to present oneself before God without any masks, or veils, or non-existent virtues, or distinctions of any kind. It is to put everything before him, including our inability to pray.

10

❖

The half-way there question

Midway upon the journey of our life
I found myself within a forest dark...

This opening verse of Dante's *Divina Commedia* shows how
there are different ages and times in our lives and how what
we call "middle age" confronts us with the experience of com-
plexity. Very often, the sensation that comes upon us is a feeling of disorientation or of our somehow having fallen asleep
interiorly. We look around us and life seems to have become a
forest. The signposts seem to us to have become less frequent
and less obvious. The way forward now leads through branches and foliage which are difficult to get through at times. It
takes us longer to get from one point to the next when, earlier
in our lives this same journey seemed to us so direct, clear and
possible.

Jesus comes to meet us at all stages in our life, and our
meeting with him transforms each halt along the way into a
time of grace. There is, in fact, a particular grace available for

the moment through which we are now living. Jesus talks to us always.

To speak of the various stages in our lives is to speak of the questions that confront us. There are questions that arise at the beginning, others that occur half way through our lives and others that accompany the end. The following text appears right in the middle of the Gospel of St. Mark. And it contains a question that typically occurs at the mid-way point:

> Jesus went on with his disciples to the villages of Caesarea Philippi; and on the way he asked his disciples, "Who do people say that I am?" They told him, "John the Baptist; and others say, Elijah; and others one of the prophets." And he asked them, "But who do you say that I am?" Peter answered him, "You are the Christ." And he charged them to tell no one about him. (Mk 8:27-30)

Jesus had called the disciples. A relationship had developed between them. To begin with, gathering enthusiasm, great signs and success. When he first called them, Jesus had come alone to the shore of the lake (Mk 1:16). A little later, there was already a crowd (Mk 2:13). And, later still, there was such a crowd around him that things became impossible (Mk 3:7-9).

There already existed the patrimony of a history lived in common: the disciples had shared with Jesus the time spent on so many journeys, moving from place to place, meals together, entering into villages and cities, in the desert and by the lake. They had witnessed astonishing signs: Jesus' own family had followed, with astonishment, the beginning of his mission (Mk 3:20-21), the authorities were following him about, wary about his royal proclamations. They had experienced storms that were suddenly stilled, they had seen him curing people and teaching them... walking on the water and being expelled from the synagogue... He had told them extraordinary things: "To you it is given to know the mystery of the Kingdom of God" (Mk 4:11); he had told them such beautiful stories: about the seed (Mk 4:3-8), the grain of mustard (Mk 4:30-32), the farmer who slept while his seed grew to fruition (Mk 4:26-29), but now he had begun to call them fearful and lacking in faith, expecting from them a courage that they did not possess.

There were lots of contradictory ideas about who or what Jesus was. Some people were saying that he was under the power of an impure spirit; others were declaring that he was the longed-for prophet. At one time, he was being proclaimed as a good teacher, at another he was being rejected as a blasphemer. We can well imagine what was going on in the hearts of the disciples!

Until one day they are far away... away from their ordinary everyday world, away from the lake, almost on the shores of the Mediterranean. Far from Jerusalem – in Caesarea. And Jesus begins asking these questions, which are those of half way through the journey, questions to be put to grown-ups. The stage which the disciples have reached is that of a faith which is capable of making a true decision. We are no longer at the stage of initial enthusiasm: they have lived through and seen enough to give a reply that does not depend on what they have heard said, but on what they actually believe. "And you, who do you say that I am?"

It is language that enables us to understand one another and to communicate – to say things and to express ourselves. But in spite of our undoubted insertion into language, at crucial moments in our lives, we have the experience of being unable to say anything, or at any rate to say what we really think or feel. Names identify a person, but the person identified does not coincide completely with the name. For this reason, a metonymical relationship, that is, the substitution of one name for another, is of no use to us. Instead of work, for instance, we speak of undertaking or task. Instead of saying spouse or bride, we say wife. The subject aspires to a symbolic, metaphorical dimension that expresses what is at root its real truth, one that no simple name is capable of expressing. It is to this level of meaning that we are transported by Jesus' question. Jesus is not waiting for the disciples to tell him merely what their eyes see, but to articulate what they feel in their hearts.

Jesus too felt the need to be spoken about, and spoken about in depth, and in words that only those who love can say. In the rabbinic tradition, it was the disciples who questioned the Master and not the other way round. In Jesus as portrayed in Mark's Gospel, we find both situations. On several occasions, it is the disciples who ask Jesus to explain something. But it also happens (cf. Mk 3:4; 9:33) that it is Jesus who challenges his disciples or those around him. This unusual way of doing things reveals the intensity of the relationship between them. Jesus does not want a teacher-pupil relationship. He wants a sharing of life, of intimacy and destiny.

And, in fact, curiously (or not!), the disciples' reply is not at the simple metonymical level. They do not say: "You are a man." "You are Mary's son." "You are a rabbi." They realize that the question that is asked at the mid-point in the journey forces us to go further, to probe the depth of the mystery of our identity. We perceive that the reply that is given at the mid-point in the journey must shed light on the way ahead, must make a difference in our lives.

Jesus asks two questions which, in a way, draw two circles, an outer one and an inner one. What is it that one sees from the outside and what is it that one sees from the inside? What is it that one sees with one's eyes, and what is it that one perceives with one's heart? The two questions: "Who do men say that I am?" and "Who do *you* say that I am?" draw a distinction between what the crowds think and what the disciples themselves think, a distinction clearly marked by the adversative form and by the emphasis of the second question. The disciple is being asked to look in such a way as to penetrate the mystery of Jesus, to see clearly and without ambiguity.

What do we see from outside?

From the outside, we can understand an identification of Jesus with John the Baptist. The first century was a period of reforming spiritual currents. The River Jordan was a much sought-after symbolic center for those who were not in agreement with the current situation in Israel. It was not by chance that John was baptizing in the Jordan and that the ministries of John and of Jesus follow one on the other (Jesus began his ministry after John had been arrested – Mk 1:14). John in fact operated along the same lines as Jesus, and pointed him out as being mightier than he himself, who was unworthy to undo his sandals (Mk 1:7). But though the revelation of Jesus appears to make him superior to his precursor, many people thought of him as no more than a second and possibly more powerful John. This is why they say about Jesus: "It is John who has come back to life."

From the outside, we can understand an identification of Jesus with Elijah. According to a biblical tradition, Elijah was taken up to heaven. In the Judaism of Jesus' own time, it was believed that, before the Messiah appeared, Elijah would re-appear to perform an eschatological role with a view to the establishment of the Kingdom of God. Elijah's role would be that of reconciling Israel and preparing it so that, at his coming, the Lord would not destroy it because of its sin.

In the meantime, in the rabbinic tradition, Elijah had become one of the most popular figures in Jewish piety. In addition to being seen as linked with the future coming of the Messiah, he had also come to be seen as an important advocate and intercessor in difficult situations, so much so that he had become the patron of all those in trouble.

For Mark, Elijah had already come to prepare the way in the person of John, as we see in the clear allusion contained in Mark 1:2-3. But at this time, many people persisted in identifying Jesus quite simply with Elijah.

From the outside, we understand the identification of

Jesus as a prophet. In his day, it was by no means unusual, especially among the people at large, for somebody to come to be known as a prophet. A number of people had appeared in Palestine in the course of the first Christian century, either calling themselves prophets or being regarded as such. Their message ranged from the call to conversion, as in the case of John the Baptist, to the phenomenon of rebellion against the Romans. In a socio-political context such as this, the identification of Jesus as a prophet makes absolute sense. Some commentators see in this attribution of the title of prophet to Jesus a reference to the eschatological prophet mentioned in Deuteronomy 18:15, 18.

Though inadequate, this is in fact a positive assessment of Jesus which must have been shared by most of those who hurried to listen to him or to seek healing from him. In Mark's eyes, however, it was not enough, because it did not express the character of novelty or of uniqueness that the figure of Jesus assumes in this Gospel.

From the point of view of Mark's account of events, the opinions of those who did not belong to the inner circle of the disciples were clearly insufficient or incorrect as a way of describing the person of Jesus. Why, then, were they included in the text? Why did the evangelist not refer simply to the direct question Jesus put to his disciples, with the Messianic confession of Peter? Its inclusion serves to highlight the contrast between what one sees from the outside and what one sees from the inside, and makes it possible to draw attention to the decisive implications of recognizing Jesus as the Messiah.

What do we see from inside?

Jesus does not comment on the opinions of others, but questions his disciples directly about what they think of him. The way the question is formulated, distinguishing between the disciples and others, shows that Jesus is hoping for a deeper appreciation from them.

The fact that it is Peter who replies is in accordance with Mark's narrative scheme, which always highlights this particular disciple. It is he who normally speaks on behalf of the group (9:5; 10:28; 11:21). And he is always the first one mentioned when a list of their names is given. His leading role is emphasized from the beginning (1:36) to the end (16:7).

Peter's replies, however, are not absolutely certain. He expresses doubts and disagrees (8:32-33). He too will undoubtedly have to travel the pathway to the Paschal understanding of Jesus. In 14:27-31, for example, he protests that he will give his life for Jesus but, in 14:66-72, he declares that he does not know "this man." His tears are the last image that Mark's Gospel gives of him, and in this way clearly reveals that it was in difficulty and trial that his faith was strengthened. We can say that, in St. Mark, Peter is, in a sense, portrayed as the prototype of the disciple, not only because of those positive attributes (which are clearly the most important) but also as a paradigmatic figure of the difficulties that need to be overcome in order to follow Jesus.

The disciple is called to see more deeply, not to be content with what he or she hears being said but rather is impelled to take up a position. The Gospel does not portray an understanding of Jesus as something that happens immediately, instantly and infallibly. It is something that slowly grows to maturity in the heart of our faith. We are feeling our way forward, always seeing the truth a bit more clearly. It is not by chance that Mark's Gospel has been called the Gospel of the Way. Finding Jesus is an extended story. It is our own story. We need humility and confidence, those qualities which prompted Cardinal Newman to dedicate to Jesus the following prayer:

> Lead, Kindly Light, amid the encircling gloom,
> Lead Thou me on!
> The night is dark, and I am far from home –
> Lead Thou me on!
> Keep Thou my feet; I do not ask to see
> The distant scene – one step enough for me.
>
> I was not ever thus, nor pray'd that Thou
> Should'st lead me on.
> I loved to choose and see my path; but now
> Lead Thou me on!
> I loved the garish day, and, spite of fears,
> Pride ruled my will: remember not past years.
>
> So long Thy power hath blest me, sure it still
> Will lead me on,
> O'er moor and fen, o'er crag and torrent, till
> The night is gone;
> And with the morn those angel faces smile
> Which I have loved long since, and lost awhile.

A reply to keep silent about

Jesus' final declaration, in which he asks the disciples to treat their declaration of faith as a secret comes as a surprise. "And he charged them to tell no one about him." Maybe we should ask why?

Silence makes us aware that we are still at an exploratory stage; we are still on the way. For now, the disciples cannot understand the full meaning of the words they had uttered, because these will only become clear in the light of the full destiny of Jesus, when the mystery of his Passover takes place. In the meantime, the disciples are forbidden to proclaim Jesus openly, but when the whole Easter mystery has taken place they will be authorized witnesses. It is important to realize that everything has to pass through the Paschal mystery of Jesus.

But the silence that Jesus calls for also has a spiritual significance: the one who loves knows that what love calls for, above all, is that one must learn to keep the secret of what one loves. In love, we say to each other: to keep your secret is my secret. The order of secrecy demands, for the mid-way question, the horizon and experience of love. We are called upon to keep the secret of Jesus and to allow this secret to form us profoundly and vitally. Meister Eckhart's advice is as follows:

> There must be silence where this presence needs to be perceived. There is no better way of reaching it than by silence; it is there that we understand things correctly: in ignorance! When we no longer

know anything, it [this presence] allows itself to be perceived and reveals itself [...]. It is by starting from knowledge that we must arrive at the state of un-knowing! For this is a superior form of knowledge.

"And you, who do *you* say that I am?" Jesus asked.

11

❖

Emmaus, laboratory of paschal faith

That very day two of them were going to a village
named Emmaus, about seven miles from Jerusalem,
and talking with each other about all these things
that had happened. While they were talking and
discussing together, Jesus himself drew near and
went with them. But their eyes were kept from recognizing him. And he said to them, "What is this
conversation which you are holding with each other as you walk?" And they stood still, looking sad.
Then one of them, named Cleopas, answered him,
"Are you the only visitor to Jerusalem who does not
know the things that have happened there in these
days?" And he said to them, "What things?" And
they said to him, "Concerning Jesus of Nazareth,
who was a prophet mighty in deed and word before
God and all the people, and how our chief priests
and rulers delivered him up to be condemned to
death, and crucified him. But we had hoped that

he was the one to redeem Israel. Yes, and besides all this, it is now the third day since this happened. Moreover, some women of our company amazed us. They were at the tomb early in the morning and did not find his body; and they came back saying that they had even seen a vision of angels, who said that he was alive. Some of those who were with us went to the tomb, and found it just as the women had said; but him they did not see." And he said to them, "O foolish men, and slow of heart to believe all that the prophets have spoken! Was it not necessary that the Christ should suffer these things and enter into his glory?" And beginning with Moses and all the prophets, he interpreted to them in all the scriptures the things concerning himself. So they drew near to the village to which they were going. He appeared to be going further, but they constrained him, saying, "Stay with us, for it is toward evening and the day is now far spent." So he went in to stay with them. When he was at table with them, he took the bread and blessed, and broke it, and gave it to them. And their eyes were opened and they recognized him; and he vanished out of their sight. They said to each other, "Did not our hearts burn within us while he talked to us on the road, while he opened to us the scriptures?" And they rose that same hour and returned to Jerusalem; and they found the eleven gathered together and those who were with them, who said, "The Lord has risen

indeed, and has appeared to Simon!" Then they
told what had happened on the road, and how he
was known to them in the breaking of the bread.
(Lk 24:13-35)

What does the Emmaus experience represent? Two disciples attempt to get away from it all, disheartened by what
appears to be the outcome of this story, the one that had
aroused such high hopes in them ("We had hoped that he was
the one to redeem Israel" Lk 24:21), but which has now made
them "sad" and not knowing what to think. The evangelist
gives the name of one of them, "the one named Cleopas" (v.
18), but this is not enough to do away with their anonymity,
a fact which may well indicate a universalizing intention on
the part of the author: those two were simply "disciples," in
other words, they represented any disciple when confronted
by Paschal faith.

It was on the road that this story began (vv. 13-27). Two
of the disciples were going to a village about seven miles from
Jerusalem. They are joined by Jesus. However, according to
the way the story is told, the eyes of the disciples are kept
from recognizing him, but not those of the reader, who knows
from the beginning the identity of the third traveler. This information is the key. Contrary to what the disciples think, the
essence of the problem is not the situation concerning Jesus:
the real problem is their own situation. It is not Jesus who had
disappeared, it was they who had not learned how to find him
and to recognize him, entrapped as they were in their lack of
information which continues to prevent them from accepting

the paschal condition of Jesus. It is worthwhile having a close look at the words that are used. The verb "to keep from," as it is used by the writers of the Synoptic Gospels, describes the hardening of the heart and is normally attributed to Jesus' adversaries. Even the disciples have to overcome their hardness of heart. The second verb, "recognize" implies a knowledge which combines not only the intimate but also the affective dimension.

When they set out from Jerusalem, the disciples did not leave behind the things that had happened there. They will be called upon, yes, to move away from the initial reading that they had made of these events. The paschal hermeneutic presupposes an internal readjustment, a critical distancing of oneself in relation to one's own ideas and opinions. It presupposes Emmaus. The two disciples could see Jesus, but they did not recognize him because their way of looking was still pre-paschal. They needed that narrative catechesis which Jesus himself gave them, that experience of intimacy which comes about as they return to the Way, the Word and the Table, where the bread is broken.

It is Jesus who takes the initiative. He joins them on the road (v. 15) and begins a conversation with them (v. 17) which deliberately breaks into the conversation between the two disciples (v. 14). The break caused by Jesus is confirmed by the reaction of the two disciples. "They stood still, looking sad" and, for the first time, they mention Jesus ("Jesus of Nazareth, who was a prophet mighty in deed and word before God and all the people"). As they describe the impression they had of Jesus, they give a brief summary of the Gospel. They begin by referring to him as being from Nazareth, which sends us back to the episodes in which the connection with Nazareth was gone into. The paradigmatic episode was that of the synagogue in Nazareth (Lk 4:16-30), where Jesus began his ministry. It was there too that Jesus proclaimed his identity and his fellow citizens did not acknowledge him. The two disciples then go on to speak of Jesus as a prophet, a title which occurred frequently to describe the pre-paschal ministry of Jesus. For example, in the section of St. Luke's Gospel that runs from 4:14 to 9:50 alone, the word prophet is used nine times and is uttered either by Jesus himself or by others. The two disciples end their account with yet another reference to the power of the deeds and words of Jesus throughout his messianic ministry.

It is then that we get a description of the "impediment" itself, which was blocking the disciples' understanding of things to such an extent:

> We had hoped that he was the one to redeem Israel. Yes, and besides all this, this is the third day since this happened. Moreover, some women of our company amazed us. They were at the tomb early in the morning and did not find his body; and they came back saying that they had even seen a vision of angels, who said that he was alive. Some of those who were with us went to the tomb, and found it just as the women had said; but him they did not see. (vv. 21-24)

Notice the importance that is given to seeing in the three happenings. The women have a vision of angels. They do not see Jesus, but they were in contact with heavenly messengers who told them that Jesus was alive. And the disciples saw what the women had told them about the tomb, but they did not see Jesus. This drama of seeing/not seeing rests on the sign of opposites. The tomb is a place that is the opposite of life. It is as if what is required is to pass over into a different place, a place of life, in order for Jesus to reveal himself as alive. And this is something that all the disciples have to discover.

Inability to see or to believe?

If what the disciples had to say enables the reader to enter into their disappointed hopes, now it is Jesus himself who makes himself known in what is clearly intended as self-revelation. For this reason, Jesus has to distance himself from their limited vision of things: "O foolish men, and slow of heart to believe all that the prophets have spoken!" (v. 25). At the beginning of the episode, the narrator informed us of the impediment suffered by the disciples: they could not see. Now the narrator leaves it to Jesus himself to reveal the principal reason for the disciples' blindness: their inability to believe. "Was it not necessary that the Christ/Messiah should suffer these things and so enter into his glory?" (v. 26).

From this point onwards, the narrative gathers speed. The mysterious stranger explains the Scriptures to the two disciples. As Michel de Certeau has said: "It is Christ who explains Christ to us." This will be a key moment in the conversion of the two disciples. They themselves put it into words: "Did not our hearts burn within us while he talked to us on the road, while he opened to us the scriptures?" (v. 32). Their hearts were purified, prepared to accept the paschal novelty.

From road to house, from house to table

The reasons that the disciples give in order to persuade Jesus to remain with them appear at first sight to be very valid: "It is toward evening and the day is now far spent" (v. 29). And they press their invitation: "Stay with us." The account gives us no details about the house nor does it even assure us that it belonged to one of the two disciples. Nevertheless, this invitation stresses a high degree of intimacy. Jesus ceases to be a stranger. The appeal to him to remain denotes a desire for relationship and hospitality.

Houses in Luke's Gospel are places where Jesus prefers to conduct his ministry of revelation. The house even comes to represent an alternative to the Temple, and all that the Temple symbolized. In the Gospel, the center of the house is the table and in this episode too, Jesus' movement is in this direction: "When he was at table with them" (v. 30). Now it is precisely at table, in the Emmaus story, that the surprise comes. Normally, a house is associated with those to whom it belongs, and it is the master of the house who presides at meals. Here we have something different. Throughout the episode so far, Jesus' actions were described in parallel with those of the two disciples. Here the disciples remain suspended, so to speak. Verse 30 is the only moment in the story in which the action belongs exclusively to Jesus ("When he was at table with them, he took the bread and blessed and broke it and gave it to them"). The one who had been the stranger has become the host. The one who was dead invites them to share his life.

The sequence of Jesus' gestures at table makes it clear that he not only takes the bread but that he gives himself in that bread, in the gesture that refers back to the total giving at the crucial moment on the cross. As a result, the narrative is changed completely. At last the disciples understand that they are continually in the presence of Jesus by the gift of Paschal faith.

Is Emmaus a new beginning?

Xavier Thévenot gives us a stimulating reading by the way he compares Luke 24 with Genesis 1-3: the Emmaus story is indeed a new Genesis. In Genesis, the creation comes about through the word of God ("God said: 'Let there be light' and there was light. God called the light 'day,' and the darkness 'night.'… God said: 'Let there be a firmament.' And it was so. God said…" – Gn 1:1-31). Here, too, Jesus opens the meaning of Scripture, he who is the Word of God. This enables him to withdraw the disciples from the deceptive plane of signs, forcing them to move from the desire to see to the desire to believe. But whereas Genesis describes a failure to meet (when Adam and Eve's eyes are opened they perceive that they are naked – Gn 3:7), Emmaus portrays a meeting, a restoration with a view to intimacy and the certainty of faith.

The restoration is brought about by the return of the disciples to Jerusalem. It was the inability to see Jesus that had prompted their departure in the first place. Their recognition of Jesus in that house, and in the Eucharistic gesture at that table, now prompts them to return. And here we encounter the Eleven and those who had remained with them in Jerusalem. The reunited community is portrayed as an anticipation and confirmation of the experience which the two from Emmaus have come to relate. Even before they speak, they acknowledge the faith proclaimed by the assembled group: "The Lord has risen indeed, and has appeared to Simon" (v. 34). Their eyes, like our own eyes, have been opened by faith.

12

❖

Pilgrims rather than travelers

The travel writer Bruce Chatwin, who wrote a great deal about the spirit of a journey, admitted in his *Anatomy of Restlessness* that the key question from which to begin is this: "Why do people move about instead of remaining settled in one place?" As we shall see, this question takes us back to the mystery of the human being.

"Why do people move about instead of remaining settled in one place?" Journeys are not merely something external. It is not only over the map of the world that a person travels. To do this would be not to recognize the essence of the human being, for example, not to identify in this restlessness which takes possession of us in the summer months a longing for something else, to go further. To move from one place to another implies a change of position, a maturing of one's vision of things, an opening out to what is new, an adapting to realities and languages, an encounter, a dialogue whether strained or dazzled, which necessarily leaves very deep impressions. The experience of a journey is a frontier experience and one of opening out that human beings need in order to be themselves. In this sense, the journey is a vital stage in the discovery and construction of ourselves and of the world. It is our consciousness that travels, discovers every detail of the world and looks at everything afresh as if seeing it for the first time. A journey is a kind of propeller for this new view of things. For this reason, it is capable of introducing into our lives and into our view of things, into the way our lives are organized, ever new elements which can bring about that radical re-textualization which, in the Christian vocabulary, we call "conversion."

Faith is a journey and leads us to it. Abraham was a traveler. Moses discovered his vocation and his mission as a command to become a wanderer. Many of the Israelite prophets, from Elijah to Jonah, lived as exiles and had been banished. Jesus himself had nowhere to lay his head (Lk 9:58), living and giving meaning to being constantly on the move. His disciples were sent out as missionaries to the four corners of the world (Mt 28:18-20):

> Jesus came and said to them: "All authority in heaven and on earth has been given to me. Go therefore and make disciples of all nations, baptizing them in the name of the Father and of the Son and of the Holy Spirit, teaching them to observe all that I have commanded you; and lo, I am with you always, to the close of the age."

Instead of travelers, we discover that we are pilgrims

This is what Paul teaches us. His personal story clearly contains a secret, something that happens precisely "as he journeyed" (Ac 9:3), as he was reaching the end of a journey which was to turn into something completely different as a result of the encounter with Jesus.

In the Letter to the Galatians, Paul gives us a first-person account of this encounter, and does so in an extraordinarily detached but nonetheless intense way, describing it as a call, a summons that originated in his mother's womb, in the same way as had happened to some of the prophets. Clearly, we are dealing here with a mystical experience, which is described in the terms in which a pious Jew would perceive such an experience. "But when he who had set me apart before I was born, and had called me through his grace, was pleased to reveal his Son to me, in order that I might preach him among the Gentiles..." (Gal 1:15-16). Paul was thinking in particular of the Books of Isaiah (49:1) and of Jeremiah (1:5), and from the beginning perceives his own destiny as a calling. In order to explain this happening, Paul uses a verb which means "God discovered in me what had lain hidden and revealed it."

Is it possible to begin a journey flat on the ground?

For this is how Paul's journey, which is also our own, began. The Acts of the Apostles recounts three times the experience that Paul described so synthetically in his Letter to the Galatians. Luke meditates theologically at length on this impenetrable encounter, a real compass which would continue always to guide Paul's journey. The encounter with Christ marks our own life for always. The fact that this episode is related three times, in Acts 9:1-18; 22:1-21, and 26:1-23, with microscopic but suggestive differences from one account to the next, shows the decisive importance he attached to it, which is not merely factual but in the order of meaning, it is theological. We too need to have another look, go back and review in our hearts the history of this encounter with Christ.

In Acts 9:1-18, what strikes us is the contrast between the light and the blindness of Paul. He is bathed in light and is blind and, for three days, he remains unable to see, neither eating nor drinking. It is as if all the images of God that Paul had fade away. And it is in the midst of the silence of these images that Paul opens himself to God's way, to the new revelation of God.

In the second account, in Acts 22:1-21, the key point is not so much the light but the voice, a voice which those with him did not hear, but only Paul himself. We know the importance of listening in the Biblical tradition, how listening formed the People of God of the Old Covenant and is to form the People of God in the New one.

The third account, in Acts 26:1-23, emphasizes the importance of seeing. In fact, we are dealing here not with a doctrine but with a personal encounter, experienced and seen by the apostle himself. This is not something that was perceived only by the eyes of the body, it is something that is seen, that comes to be seen with the eyes of faith, it is that movement within revelation itself.

Paul's Secret is Christ

The Christ event marks the beginning of a totally new journey in Paul's life. When Paul thinks about his own existence and of man's existence in the world, he will never be able to dissociate it from the Paschal revelation of Christ. Everything starts from Christ. He discovers that we are for Christ. It is through Christ that we are, in the Father and in the Spirit. Christ, by his death and resurrection, introduces us into a new and dynamic relationship with God. We have access to intimacy with him. The word "access" (in Greek *prosagogé*) is interesting; it occurs both in Romans 5:2 and in Ephesians 3:12. The etymology of this word is connected with the ritual in courtly life whereby the king's intimate friends were admitted to direct contact with him, something which, obviously, was not available to the majority of his subjects. Christ is the one who gives us this access to the intimacy of the Father. And it is in this light that human existence can really be spoken of as new.

Paul's life, like that of every pilgrim and traveler, is full of trials, of unexpected happenings, of setbacks. But we can be confident, as the Letter to the Ephesians (3:17-21) tells us: "That Christ may dwell in your hearts through faith; that you, being rooted and grounded in love, may have power to comprehend with all the saints what is the breadth and length and height and depth, and to know the love of Christ which surpasses knowledge, that you may be filled with all the fullness of God. Now to him who by the power at work within us is able to do far more abundantly than all that we ask or think,

to him be glory in the church and in Christ Jesus to all generations, for ever and ever. Amen."

Paul explains clearly the reason for this confidence that
we can have: it is the superabundance, the fullness, the un-
surpassable *pleroma* of the grace of Christ. We are Christ's
associates and our existence becomes a Christ-like existence.
For this reason, Paul's whole theology is based on a description of the transformations that take place in people in their
journey to God in Christ. It is a real theology of a journey of
which the Cross and the Resurrection are both the map and
the route, the thirst and the fountain. "It is no longer I who
live, it is Christ who lives in me" (Gal 2:20).

When we undertake a pilgrimage, we often ask ourselves
where it will end, because one of the things that one experiences is that as we proceed on our way, reality becomes ever
more open. When the pilgrim reaches the point of perceiving
things in his or her heart, then it is that things really begin.
The pilgrimage does not really have an end: it has an extraordinary purpose. Paul's is Christ. So, too, is ours.

13

❖

The Magnificat: perhaps the most beautiful poem

There are two Christian writers who have commented in a most original way on the *Magnificat*. I will begin with them. The first one, Paul Claudel, lost his faith as a young man. It was, we might say, a faith that he had inherited, sociological.... His discovery of God, the conversion that was to transform him completely, happened much later, on a day when, almost by chance, he had gone into Notre Dame Cathedral in Paris and heard the *Magnificat* being sung. Claudel has described what he felt: "All of a sudden, my heart was moved as never before; I believed within myself and with all my strength; my whole being was as it were violently caught up to the Heights. And there was in me such a strong conviction, an indescribable sureness that caused all my earlier doubts to disappear."

Next, the commentary made almost accidentally by Sophia de Mello Andresen, one of the most important Portuguese-speaking poets. In an interview published in a cultural review, she said: "I often think that the *Magnificat* is possibly the most beautiful poem there is. It is a poem that 'proclaims,' and does not simply hymn the earth as Homer did. Between two worlds, at the crossroads of history, a woman stands and proclaims the poem of Salvation."

We need to look with fresh eyes at this text which is often the prisoner of routine but which, in itself, is an inexhaustible spring of jubilant spiritual life.

When she accepted the message of the Angel, Mary expressed her consent in an astonishingly brief phrase (she did not fall into our temptation of making long speeches about everything). All she said was: "Behold, the handmaid of the Lord; be it done to me according to your word" (Lk 1:38). Through the *Magnificat,* Mary would be able to prolong her "yes," making it clear that she knew well its profound implications. In the *Magnificat,* Mary breaks her silence and explains the meaning of her acceptance. And she does this in the simplest and most genuine way possible, interpreting first of all her own experience of faith and then anchoring herself in what the history of salvation teaches her about God and about the mission of the People of God in the world.

There are two things we can say about the *Magnificat.* It is the great summary of Mary's experience. The *Magnificat* is not a parenthesis; it presupposes everything, absolutely everything that Mary had lived through. It is impossible to get to know her without dwelling at length on these words which are the expression of her intimate thoughts concerning her destiny. If, now, she can sing that "the Lord has regarded the low estate of his handmaiden. For behold, henceforth all generations will call me blessed" (vv. 47-48), it is because she had already courageously declared herself the "handmaid" and "slave" of the Lord at the time of the Annunciation (v. 38) and Elizabeth had already greeted her as "blessed among women" (v. 42). Mary's acknowledgment that "He who is mighty had done great things in me" (v. 49) is in line with the Angel's assurance that "with God nothing is impossible" (v. 37). And though it is true that what prompts the hymn is a concrete personal experience, this quickly becomes a hymn of praise for the work of God who was, and is, in all the situations in Mary's life – as in our own – the "Savior," the "Holy One," the "Mighty One," the "Worker of Wonders," the "Merciful One." In the *Magnificat*, Mary sings her own history. And in so doing she challenges us to do the same. Nobody lives a fertile spiritual life unless and until we are capable of recognizing what we were like to begin with, unless we are able to enter into a relationship with God that is a living dialogue between an "I" and a "Thou." Mary's prayer is not a series of formulas. She reveals her life in what she says.

On the other hand, in the very strong connection that the *Magnificat* has with the biblical tradition that went before it, we can see how Mary sought nourishment and light in the Word of God. Her experience of faith does not push her into a closed and self-regarding circuit, but places her in an openness to what went before and to what will come afterwards: she seeks confirmation in the faith journey of the People of God and feels supported by the great models of faith. Both the overall structure of the *Magnificat* and the ideas expressed in it, even down to the phrases and words used, reflect passages that have already been spoken, already experienced in the Old Testament. The entire *Magnificat* is a real mosaic of earlier biblical expressions. And this is not plagiarism, it is to feel that our faith history is both fed by and is a continuation of other stories.

For this reason, the important thing is not so much to identify the particular episode or passages in the Old Testament that may have served as inspiration for the *Magnificat*, because what is difficult is not to be able to find a phrase that corresponds exactly to each of those in the *Magnificat*. What is fruitful spiritually is to be aware of the way in which Mary, in her Canticle, stands out as a perfect representative of people who believe. She bears witness to the fact that God really does love human beings, that God is faithful to the lives of men and women, that his promises are kept. From this point of view, the one who proclaims the *Magnificat* is a genuine icon of the People of God on the way.

Her prayer is absolutely hers, because it refers to the concrete facts of her own history, but these extraordinary events are also set within a wider communitarian framework. This is, in fact, what one hopes for from all prayer: the possibility, on the one hand, for it to be formulated, as the *Magnificat* was, in the first-person singular; but at the same time, on the other hand, for this particular concrete history to be linked with the wider horizon of God's plans and mission for the community of believers.

We perceive that the Canticle of the *Magnificat* is uniquely linked with the Gospel of St. Luke. The first part of the Gospel, known as the "Infancy Narrative," contains a number of songs: the Canticle of Zechariah, father of John the Baptist, the song of Elizabeth as she welcomes Mary; the song of the angels in announcing the birth of Jesus, and the Canticle of Simeon. All of these reveal how the great theme of St. Luke's Gospel is salvation and how the experience of salvation puts us on our feet, fills us with irrepressible enthusiasm and makes us sing.

Now, the first explicit reference to salvation that occurs in the Gospel is precisely in the *Magnificat,* in Mary's description of God as being her *Savior* (1:47). And since the *Magnificat* appears in the first chapter of the Gospel, we clearly perceive the desire to establish a link between the beginning of the Gospel and the end of the Acts of the Apostles (which, as we know, was also written by St. Luke), in which it is stated that God's salvation had also been sent to the Gentiles (Ac 28:23-28). In other words, each part of the Gospel, and the entire work taken as a whole, aim to do nothing other than show how salvation is passed on, amplified, and propagated. Thus the *Magnificat* has a real programmatic function. It is not simply a passage or a section of Luke's Gospel: It really enables us to reconstitute and to touch the meaning of the whole.

The *Magnificat* can be divided into three parts, like a poem which speaks not only of a particular incident in the life of Mary, but as a reflection of her entire life.

1) In verses 46-49, Mary sings of her personal vocation.

"My soul magnifies the Lord, [47] and my spirit rejoices in God my Savior, [48] For he has looked on the humble estate of his servant. For behold, from now on all generations will call me blessed. [49] For he who is mighty has done great things for me, and holy is his name."

2) In verses 50-53, Mary realizes that the love of God which she has experienced is not different from the way God acts throughout the history of salvation.

[50] "And his mercy is for those who fear him from generation to generation. [51] He has shown strength with his arm; he has scattered the proud in the thoughts of their hearts. [52] He has brought down the mighty from their thrones and exalted those of humble estate. [53] He has filled the hungry with good things, and the rich he has sent away empty."

3) In verses 54-55, Mary recognizes that her vocation is linked with and is inserted into the mission of the People of God.

[54] "He has helped his servant Israel, in remembrance of his mercy, [55] as he spoke to our fathers, to Abraham and to his offspring forever."

1ª) Mary sings of what she is, her personal vocation (vv. 46-49)

The *Magnificat* is a hymn of praise. "O sing a new song to the Lord" (Ps 95[6]:1), exhorts the psalmist. The Book of Job says that the Creator God wishes to be celebrated "when the morning stars sing together, and all the sons of God shout for joy" (Job 38:7). In the first Covenant with Moses, both Moses himself and the children of Israel sang to the Lord after they had crossed the Red Sea. Miriam, Moses' sister, took the initiative, and other women emerged, following her, singing: "Sing to the Lord, for he has triumphed gloriously, the horse and his rider he has thrown into the sea" (Ex 15:21). The People of God was discovering that it was so loved and protected by God that it could only sing. David who, the biblical text tells us, was king according to God's heart, "danced with all his might" before the Ark of the Covenant in a procession that included harps, lutes, tambourines and cymbals. The Acts of the Apostles record that Paul and Silas, when they realized that God was releasing them from prison because he has a saving plan for them, also began to sing (Ac 16:25ff.). And in the Book of Revelation, in a meditation on the Church's vocation and mission, the Christians walk "beside a sea of glass, singing: 'Great and wonderful are thy deeds, O Lord God the Almighty! Just and true are thy ways, O King of the ages!'" (Rv 15:2-3).

Why does Mary sing? Perhaps the most beautiful answer to this question is given to us in a verse by St. John of the Cross: "All those who are in love sing"! Mary sings because she is in love. It is very important to realize that Mary's prayer in particular does not consist in ideas but in facts. Mary's prayer is neither impersonal nor abstract. It bursts out from the most intense, most vehement and most committed center of her being. The silent and obedient "servant of the Lord" here breaks out into songs of praise, though she is not praising herself but the God who saves. There is a well-known story about an Indian, in America, who was criticizing the greediness for possessions and the egoism of "the whites" and who said that "white men make God poorer." Mary's canticle and her attitude are the very opposite. She magnifies, that is she makes God great, with all the energy that she finds in herself and that radiates from her.

Mary recognizes her littleness before the greatness of God; and it is because she recognizes it that she can also rejoice. To place our naked lives, whole and entire in all their littleness, in God's hands in no way diminishes us. St. Paul was to write, along the lines of the *Magnificat*, "When I am weak, then I am strong" because the grace of God is all we need (2 Cor 12:10). At times we ask ourselves what it is that we need. What else do we need so that we can be happy? What do we need so that others can consider us fortunate? And we easily live in this insatiable anxiety. Mary in the *Magnificat* teaches us that we do not need anything, none of us needs anything in order for us to be able to be set on fire and transformed by the grace of God. God simply loves us for no reason at all; he loves us because he loves us. Contrary to what we tend to think, the weakness that we find within ourselves is not an obstacle to his love. Let us allow God to love our littleness, our insignificance, our emptiness, our nothingness. Only this will enable us really to open wide our doors to God and then he will be able say that our vocation, whatever it is, will be Love.

2ª) Mary's vocation to Love is confirmed by the loving ways of God in history (vv. 50-53)

In the first part, Mary declared that God had wrought in her a new creation, on the basis of her nothingness. The second part of the *Magnificat* (vv. 53-56) is a demonstration of the proof of this fact when one reflects on the way in which God had acted throughout the history of salvation. God acted thus in Mary, because it is thus that God always acts. The Creator God, the Almighty Lord, reveals in all times and to the fullest extent in Jesus that his power is Love and Mercy. Mary, daughter of the People of the Covenant, points to this characteristic of God both in the concrete history of Israel and in the history of her own vocation. As had happened with herself, similarly down through the generations, God acted lovingly on behalf of the poor, of the little ones, of the most neglected. Jesus was himself to celebrate this in the form of a canticle in Matthew 11:25: "I thank you, Father, Lord of heaven and earth, that you have hidden these things from the wise and understanding and revealed them to babes." This is how it always is. Hence we are called to trust above all in the goodness and mercy of God. As the theologian Dietrich Bonhoeffer used to say: "God does not give us everything we want, but He is faithful and keeps all his promises." Mary is a model because she believed, with unshakeable faith, in the power and immediacy of God's Mercy.

This brings us to vv. 51-53 of the *Magnificat*. Mary, expressing concretely the functioning of God's Mercy, prays: "He has shown strength with his arm; he has scattered the proud in the thoughts of their hearts. He has brought down the mighty from their thrones and exalted those of humble estate. He has filled the hungry with good things, and the rich he has sent away empty." The salvation which God comes to ensure for all does not ignore the concrete situations of particular people: as there is personal sin and social sin (which is related to sinful social structures), so, too, conversion is individual and, at the same time, involves implications and commitments with a view to the transformation of the world according to justice and love. As the First Letter of St. John was later to say (1 Jn 4:20): "If anyone says, 'I love God,' and hates his brother, he is a liar; for he who does not love his brother whom he has seen, cannot love God whom he has not seen." Christianity introduces into history a tension of love, justice and truth. All stand before the power of God. He is Lord. All are dependent on him. And if the *Magnificat* hymns the transformation that God can bring about, it is in order to state clearly that we are all in God's hands. In his letter concerning the new Millennium, *Novo Millennio Ineunte,* John Paul II challenged the Church of our own day, the Church which we are, to rediscover the "creativity of charity." This means to devote our energy, creativity, wisdom and enthusiasm in seeking solutions that express the alternative of love to which the *Magnificat* points prophetically.

3ª) Mary locates her vocation in the mission of the People of God (vv. 54-55)

The two concluding verses of the *Magnificat* are these: "He has helped his servant Israel, in remembrance of his mercy, as he spoke to our fathers, to Abraham and to his offspring forever." At the end, Mary reflects on the history of the People of God which began with the call of Abraham, to whom God had promised: "I will make of you a great nation, and I will bless you, and make your name great, so that you will be a blessing. And by you all the families of the earth shall bless themselves" (Gn 12:2-3). The *Magnificat* tells us that no one is an island. The vocation of each woman and of each man is linked with the memory and present-day relevance of the mission of the People of God. Each one of us both inherits and transmits life. Mary helps us to see how all the promises, all the dreams, all the mercies flow together in each one. God created the human being so that he could create you and you and you. God blessed the whole of creation so that you, every time the sun rises and every time it sets, might feel blessed. God heard the tears and lamentations of his people in Egypt, in order to be able, today, to hear your own distress and your cry for help. God inspired the prophets so that today you would be given the words of consolation and hope that you need. God caused his Son to be born as man so that you could today be born closer to God.

And, at the same time, Mary locates herself at the edge of the new age, as the dawn of a new and much wider hope of which she herself is the transmitter. She is the image of the Church on the way, protectress and intercessor for the Church. Here, too, bursts forth a fundamental challenge for us: the challenge to live by giving life, to overcome the individualism so dominant in our culture, and to view our lives as a service and dedication to others. We only lose what we do not give to others.

ST PAULS

This book was produced by ST PAULS, the publishing house operated by the Society of St. Paul, an international religious congregation of priests and brothers dedicated to serving the Church through the communications media.

For information regarding this and associated ministries of the Pauline Family of Congregations, write to the Vocation Director, Society of St. Paul, 2187 Victory Blvd., Staten Island, New York 10314-6603. Phone (718) 982-5709; or E-mail:vocation@stpauls.us or check our internet site, www.vocationoffice.org

That the Word of God be everywhere known and loved.